# ADVANCE PRAISE

"This deeply moving book is a courageous exposure of Jana's deepest childhood wounding. It ripens and brims with compelling prose and authenticity, as we follow her success in integrating and healing her inner child in this empowering, confessional prescriptive memoir."
—Kate Robinson, *The US Review of Books* Recommended

"In this debut memoir, Jana Wilson courageously shares her path to healing childhood trauma. Wise Little One is an intimate portrait of perseverance and spirituality."

—*Kirkus Reviews*

"Wilson's evocative and descriptive prose doesn't shy from the dark side of domestic violence in her home. Wilson takes the reader through a vivid journey of seeking and lasting healing, until she eventually finds it within herself with her Wise Little One. An Inspiring memoir about healing from childhood trauma."

—*BookLife Publishers Weekly*

"Jana Wilson sacredly tells the story of her heart's healing journey out of the darkness with bravery, honesty & humility. The result is a powerful, inspiring and transformational navigation through childhood trauma and into the present moment that invites us to shine a light on our own shadows, free ourself from their grip, and truly step into our power. Jana boldly holds up the mirror and brilliantly guides us by example with tender grace and fearless authenticity. *Wise Little One* is a real-world blueprint for how to achieve emotional freedom regardless of the wounds of your past."

—davidji, author of *Sacred Powers*

"I have no doubt that many will find themselves in Jana's story but what I loved the most about this book was Jana's complete honesty. This kind of honesty is only possible when we have truly met the parts of ourselves that we have been conditioned to avoid and all the feelings and emotions that we'd rather push aside like shame or guilt."

—Maggie Gilewicz, PhD
Author of *How To Make Sure Your Life Doesn't Suck: A Different Kind Of Guide To Navigating The Ups And Downs Of Life*

"Inner child work has seemed theoretical to me in the past, without a way of actually practicing it. Jana's book taught me how to do that through tangible steps and through her own story of meeting this part of herself. My relationship with my inner child has already deepened as a result of this profound book, and I'm enjoying the peace and safety it has offered me! Give yourself the gift of nurturing this beautiful aspect of yourself and get this book!"

—Emily Smith, Author of *Wholeness Within: Insights from One Woman's Journey of Creating a Life and Career in Alignment*

"With her heartfelt anecdotes and practical advice, Jana offers invaluable tools for self-reflection, self-care, and cultivating a loving relationship with the inner child. She demonstrates how to overcome the past and manifest an inspiring future by harnessing the power of self-compassion, forgiveness, and resilience. The story of Jana Wilson resonates deeply with anyone who has experienced trauma, providing a guiding light for reclaiming joy, authenticity, and the ability to manifest an inspiring life filled with love. I give Wise Little One five stars!

—Michelle Kidwell, Author & Book Blogger

"The scenes are vivid, the characters complex and well-developed, the pacing, the momentum, the drama all come together to create a compelling narrative. Jana wasn't afraid of telling the truth about her family and herself, even when that truth must have been hard to share with readers."

—Andy Ross, Ross Literary Agency

# Wise Little One

*Learning to Love and Listen to My Inner Child*

A Memoir

**by *Jana Wilson***

Founder of Emotional Healing Systems

EHS PUBLISHING

Printed in the United States of America

I have tried to recreate events, locales, and conversations from my memories of them. To maintain anonymity in some instances, we have changed the names of individuals and places. I may have changed some identifying characteristics and details such as physical properties, occupations, and places of residence.

First Printing, 2023

ISBN 979-8-9875497-2-8 Paperback
ISBN 979-8-9875497-1-1 Hardcover
ISBN 979-8-9875497-0-4 Ebook

Library of Congress Control Number: 2023902759

Published by EHS Publishing Inc.

Book design by Asya Blue Design.

www.janawilson.com

# DEDICATION

For my beloved husband, Lance Wilson, with you by my side, there are Infinite Possibilities. Thank you for the support, encouragement, and guidance. And to my greatest teacher and my heart, my one and only daughter, Taylor Rae, I live in gratitude that you chose me to be your mom.

And to the readers of this book, my intent is to show you what is possible through learning to love and listen to YOUR inner child. Thank you for taking the time to read my stories, it is truly an honor.

# AUTHORS NOTE

One day in early 2022, I came out of my morning meditation practice and received a message from Spirit, "It's time to write the book." I've had the dream of writing my memoir for twenty-five years, attended a memoir writing retreat, read countless books on the topic. It just wasn't time. Previously anytime I sought out support to write the book, it fell flat. So, I replied to Spirit's internal nudge, "Ok, then you must give me the support I need to accomplish it." I immediately sat down at my laptop and searched for developmental editors and found a website that I had previously never found. It was just the sign I was looking for.

Over the next year, between working with clients and leading retreats, I poured my heart and soul into my past. There were many heartbreaking days that led to weeks of deeper healing. Bringing up so much of the trauma that I thought I had completely healed, was sobering. I came to fully understand that we always have another layer of healing, even when we have committed our life to healing and helping others. With the highest integrity I used my memory and the stories my Mom, Granny and other family members shared with me. Memory is an interesting phenomenon – it's subjective and not always completely accurate depending on the state of consciousness we were in when we experienced the event.

Wise Little One, is the sharing of my story, from the time in utero, to where I am today in my life. There may be triggers reading my stories, certainly if you have experienced childhood abuse, at times it may bring up those memories and resulting traumas. I don't apologize for that, for what we can't feel, we can't heal. I also use profanity as an accurate depiction of what was said. My intent is to share with the world a story that will inspire and provide a path of healing for anyone who is willing to take responsibility and do the work that deep soul healing requires.

At the end of some of the chapters I have shared knowledge on the tools I've used to heal and those I teach with the intention to support the reader on their healing journey. I have also shared the names of many of the teachers who had the most impact in my healing. Some of the names of people involved were changed and some omitted to respect their privacy.

# PROLOGUE

The grass was cold and rough beneath my bare feet. The air was cool and damp, the blistering heat of the Florida summer months now just a memory. I wrung my hands together as the muffled shouts coming from our shabby, old trailer rose and fell. I'd seen what happened before and I knew what was going to happen next. Theirs was a well-choreographed dance of screams and slaps, punches and kicks, name calling and big, angry blows.

*What, you think you're smarter than me?*

*Please, no, I'm sorry, Archie.*

*You're nothing but a Reader's Digest whore.*

*You're right, please. . .*

*Of course, I'm right, you—*

*NO, ARCHIE, NO!*

The day had started like many other days in my first twelve years of life—Dad working to get his old truck running, tossing beer can after another on the ground, eventually disappearing to get into whatever trouble he got into when he was drunk. I spent the better part of the day cleaning the trailer—sweeping floors, dusting surfaces, putting everything in its place, doing whatever I could to feel a sense of control and safety. My big brother Roy, becoming ever more independent, had left the house hours earlier to be with his friends. I couldn't blame him.

As the sun began to melt into the horizon, Dad screeched into the driveway. He stumbled inside, ambled to the kitchen, and sloshed Jack Daniels into a glass before settling at the table, ready to be served. Mom placed a heaping serving of chicken and dumplings in front of him. He sneered at her before reaching for his fork and shoveling a bite into his mouth. Immediately, he spat the food back onto the plate.

The small space closed in around me. I froze for a moment. I braced myself for what was coming next.

"What the hell is this?" he slurred.

Mom's body tensed. "It's your dinner," she replied.

He slammed his hands on the table. "It's fucking cold, that's what it is."

She reached to pull his plate closer to her, "I'm sorry, let me—"

"Let you what?" His voice rose, "MAKE ME A NEW FUCKING PLATE OF FOOD?"

Mom cowered.

Dad gripped the flimsy folding table and, in one motion, flipped it over, sending a full plate of food to the floor. Shattering ceramic and clanking silverware echoed as he lunged at Mom, his shirt grazing my face as he leapt.

I ran toward the door and burst through it, gulping the cool night air. I wanted to bolt—to start running like I did with Roy during moments like this. Roy always took the brunt of Dad's rage; he was my protector in those early years. But Roy wasn't there this time, it was only me. I had no choice but to stay and ride out the storm like a little girl lost on a raft in stormy seas.

I tried to focus on the cicadas' song; to let myself be lulled by their sweet, silky drone. But nothing could distract me from the horror of another raging fight between my emotionally stunted parents.

I turned my gaze upward. It was one of the clearest nights I had ever seen. The sky, jet black, was strewn with glistening stars, some fat and luminous, others small and subtly glinting. I squeezed my palms together and began to pray.

*Jesus, please; please help me.*

*Please, help me.*

*Please.*

Suddenly all sound faded into the background.

*I cracked my eyes.*

*I was no longer in my body.*

Instead, I found myself floating on a plane of stars flung across an endless expanse of pitch black. Confused, I looked around and saw that I was floating in the cosmos—nebulas, galaxies, and star nurseries were all around me. Cradled by clouds of vapor, so calm and tranquil. In that moment, I felt more love and peace than I had ever experienced.

As far as I was from the Earth, I could still see our dilapidated, white and maroon trailer. I could faintly hear my dad still cussing and hollering. I could even see my little self, standing in the yard, wringing my hands, shoulders tight against my ears. I stared at the Earthly version of me, feeling empathy for her fear, compassion for her pain.

*Please don't send me back.* I thought.

At that moment, I heard clearly, "Those are not your parents. I am. That is not your life. This is."

Like a baby in the arms of loving parents, I was safe. I relaxed into that Truth. I wasn't Trailer Trash Jana, daughter of two people tearing one another apart. For the first time in my life, I felt a deep knowing that everything was going to be okay. I was a Divine Child, and I wanted to feel these feelings forever. I wanted to play amongst the stars, to float and giggle, to exist here without worry about the past or the future. After all, here, softly cradled, I wasn't burdened by heartbreak, helplessness or fear. I felt safe.

*I am safe.*

*I never want to go back.*

And with that, I opened my eyes and found myself back on the spindly grass, listening to my father's roar. But now I wasn't afraid. My body softened and relaxed. I looked up at the dark sky and let out a sigh. I had been there—to a blissful place that I could only describe as Heaven. It felt like I was in a celestial playground of Infinite Possibilities. I now *knew* that I was one with God and that place was my home. Yes, there was more slamming, screaming, shattering, sobbing, and punching. But something had changed. I was no longer bound to these people who had given me life on Earth. No longer tied to the here and now. I'd experienced a more expanded state of awareness with a new understanding of the Universe, and my place in it.

*Those aren't your parents.*

*I am.*

*That isn't your life.*

*This is.*

## *Chapter 01*

# RETREAT

### ∽ *2015* ∾

*"In each of us, there is a young, suffering child. It may be that we haven't dared to face this child for many decades."*[1]

—Thich Nhat Hanh

There is a place where the forest meets the sea. Mythic in reputation, it is a salty, spectacular piece of coastline where ruthless waves beat against the shore flanked by jutting cliffs. Hot springs bubble up from the cliffside, causing steam to rise and hover just above the rock. Steep, rugged mountains rise from a place beyond the shore, providing a stark backdrop to a place of integrated healing and transformation—The Esalen Institute.

That's where I heard it—a tiny voice from within that whispered *leave*.

For the past three days, I had been in this magical place, the world-famous human potential center; a place to explore higher consciousness. I had dreamed of attending a retreat at Esalen for many years and intended

---

1 Thich Nhat Hanh, Reconciliation: Healing The Inner Child (Parallax Press, 2006)

to lead a retreat there one day. This experience was the result of years of envisioning and disciplined practices.

The week-long event was being led by Sally Kempton. She facilitates retreats that integrate meditation, yoga philosophy, and spiritual life-skills. I had previously sat in meditation with Deepak Chopra, Wayne Dyer, and Eckhart Tolle, but I had yet to experience anything like the meditations with Sally. A group of sixty of us would enter the meditation pavilion, find a spot and settle in. As we dropped our eyes, Sally guided us in hours-long meditation sessions that integrated our natural surroundings. I'd become a bird, swooping and soaring over the forest, and then, I'd be a dolphin exploring the depths of the ocean. I'd never had ethereal experiences like the ones I was having with Sally. I was locked in; deeply connected.

Yet something still whispered, *leave.*

On the second day, after our sixth hour of meditation, I went to my room and rested on my bed, staring vacantly at the ceiling. The loud, rhythmic sounds of the Pacific called me to relax. I took a deep breath and placed my hand on my heart. It was tugging at me, nudging me gently, urging me to go. With the magic that enfolded me at Esalen, I couldn't understand why I was feeling this pull. Instead of listening to that inner-voice, I wrestled with it, and eventually shoved it aside and got ready for dinner.

I walked into the dining hall in a bright yellow sundress that caught the breeze. I took a plate and piled it with delicious food made from fresh produce grown on campus. Just outside there was a sweeping lawn with a swimming pool overlooking the beautiful Big Sur coastline. Nearly everyone was naked—at Esalen, swimsuits are optional. I swallowed feelings of discomfort, wrapping an arm around my waist, adjusting my dress as I sat. The idea of public nudity caused an uncomfortable stirring in my gut. As open and free as everyone else seemed to be, I couldn't bring myself to consider it. The idea of being naked around others awakened feelings in me that were almost too much to bear: exploitation, sexualization, objectification. Those were the things my body knew.

The whisper grew louder: *leave*.

I finished my dinner, went back to my room, and got into my bathing suit. I walked the path down the hill from the Lodge to the hot springs overlooking the cliff. It was breathtaking; there was a living roof featuring crystals and a succulent garden. I hung my towel and found a communal soaking tub to ease into. The views were spectacular; the ocean crashed against the rocks below. I was the only person covered up as I dipped my toes into the hot water, then eventually submerged myself. I closed my eyes as I settled into my spot and leaned my head on the rock behind me. Nearby, a couple were moaning, experiencing something sexual. My throat tightened. My body tensed. My breath hastened.

*Leave.*

Back in my room, I got ready for bed. Now, the whispers were loud, calling out, begging me to pay attention. Regardless of my discomfort over public nudity, I was right in the middle of a once-in-a-lifetime experience. I couldn't go. There was just no way. As I crawled into my bed and drew the covers up to my chin, I noticed something. My joints felt sore, I had painful pressure in my sinuses, my body felt *off*. I fell into a restless sleep that night, tossing and turning as my mind fought what I was being called to do.

The next morning, I gazed out over the ocean, willing peace to come. Yet, my body felt weak; my mind tangled. I made my way to the meditation pavilion, ready for another group session with Sally. This would only be a half day and we'd be given the rest of the day off. During every other session, once I dropped my eyes, I was able to stay in meditation for hours at a time. Today, I couldn't escape the discomfort. My body ached; my mind was haunted. Over and over again, I heard it.

*Leave.*

The meditation seemed to drag this time. I couldn't work with my thoughts the way I typically could. My experience was choppy—different. Just as Sally was wrapping things up, I reminded myself of what I know and what I teach. This is why I practice meditation; to listen to that still, small voice. I'd spent my entire life learning to connect with my Spiritual guidance and to my inner child. I knew it was vital to maintain that connection. The inner child is our feeling self. It is the part of us that communicates to us through our emotions. I affectionately call mine Little Jana:

*Wise Little One.*

At that moment, it all became clear. Little Jana needed something, and it was my responsibility to listen. With this realization, I didn't hesitate. I gathered my things and hurried out, making a scene as I tiptoed over people and bolted out of the hall. I ran toward my room to pack my bag. My joints ached, my head pounded, I wanted nothing more than to escape. I jumped into my rental car, turned the key, and pulled out of the parking lot, never stopping to grieve as Esalen disappeared in my rearview mirror. I headed north on the Pacific Coast Highway, driving alongside the ocean. As I drove, the flu-like symptoms I'd been feeling vanished, replaced by a deep sense of comfort. My mind, body and soul were braided and had worked together to get me to listen. Now, I was tuned in. My Wise Little One was speaking to me and I was hearing her loud and clear.

"Okay," I said aloud. "Where would you like to go?"

I heard, *forest.*

I drove twenty-five minutes to Pfeiffer State Park and got out of my car. I walked onto a trail where I saw a towering 1,200-year-old redwood named Colonial Tree. I made my way over to the tree and placed my hand on its massive trunk; I was in awe. It was bold and powerful, its energy steady and strong. Being in its presence brought me a sense of stability and grounding. In an instant, I felt rooted.

I sat on the ground, at the base of the tree and began to cry. I leaned into the discomfort, operating as a loving adult to my inner child, asking her, "What story am I telling you that has you feeling so sad"?

As tears slid down my face, I became acutely aware of a familiar pattern, here I was, 49 years-old and internally terrorizing myself, worried

I would end up like my mom—alone. I desired someone to share my life with. I longed for my man; my beloved, who would co-create a miraculous life with me. I spent nearly an hour resting by the ancient redwood, until finally, a sense of peace washed over me.

I finally stood, wiped the dirt from my bottom, my face puffy from the tears, and got back into my car. I pulled out of the park onto the highway and drove north until I arrived at an inn overlooking Monterey Bay. I checked in and immediately went out on to the balcony to sit for my afternoon meditation practice. Stillness and silence enveloped me, my mind settled, my heart became coherent. I took a cleansing breath; a cool breeze caressed my face.

As my practice ended, I opened my eyes, stared over the bay, and asked the question to Little Jana again, "Where would you like to go now?"

Instantly, I heard—*Carmel.*

I took a quick shower, threw on a dress, dabbed some gloss on my lips and pulled my hair back in a ponytail. I got in the car, and began my drive down the coast, watching waves crash against the shore as I made my way toward the idyllic town of Carmel-by-the-Sea. I noticed birds hovering and sinking into the water, eager for food. The ocean repeated the cycle: ebb and flow.

When I arrived in Carmel, the sun was beginning its descent. I intentionally parked a good distance from my favorite restaurant—The Flying Fish—so I could stroll through the town. Carmel is one of my favorite places in the world. It is a quintessential coast meets mountain village. The mornings bring a foggy marine layer that hugs the coastline and cypress trees, while the evenings bring cool, clear breezes. The streets are lined with gently sloping green sod, wooden roofs. Many of the cottages are adorned with window boxes filled with lush red and purple fuchsias that spill over the sides. It's like living in a fairytale. I was enchanted. This place reminded me of somewhere I'd always wanted to live. I draped a cashmere scarf over my shoulders and wandered slowly, tuning into Little Jana as I walked, letting myself take in the salty air and spectacular views. She was ecstatic.

I arrived at the entrance to The Flying Fish and ducked inside. The hostess got me settled at a table and handed me a menu. After a quick glance, I sipped my water and looked around at all the couples having dinner, chatting quietly, looking lovingly into one another's eyes. I began the habitual, damaging self-talk...

*What do these people have that I don't?*

*Will I ever meet my beloved?*

After so many days of silence, I was able to quickly catch the thoughts. Immediately I made amends with myself for comparing myself to others and entertaining an old false belief I held—*I'm unwanted*.

I whispered to myself, "I'm sorry. Please forgive me. I love you. Thank you." Part of Huna, a healing tradition passed down through generations of Hawaiian indigenous peoples, this prayer is called Ho'oponopono. It literally means 'to make right'.

I turned my attention back to the present moment and stared across the table in awe. Clear as day, there sat Little Jana, my Wise Little One, a sweet, brown-eyed, 5-year-old girl with wispy blond hair, staring back at me. She smiled. My heart rate began to quicken. What happened next was nothing short of miraculous; I left my body. Getting my bearings, I was aware I was looking at my grownup self through her eyes. What she showed me reminded me of the poem by Rumi:

"By God, when you see your beauty, you will be the idol of yourself."[2]

Little Jana gently guided me to see the badass I had become. She showed me all that I had courageously conquered and the choices that had led me to this moment in time—I had arrived. She reminded me that I enjoyed success in most areas of my life. My career was at a peak, the emotional healing system I had created was making a real difference in the lives of my clients. My physical health was optimal. The only thing missing was my man; my partner; my beloved. With that thought, I felt heartache.

---

2 Rumi, *The Essential Rumi*, ed. Coleman Barks (Harper Collins, 1995)

I had been abandoning Little Jana every time I entertained narratives about being alone and unwanted. It was a lie. In a flash of wisdom, I knew I was whole, I was complete, there was no place to get to, no higher place to climb. I had arrived in this present moment when, truly, all was well. I'd wrestled with the idea of being alone for so long, that I never stopped to question that story. There, sitting in a booth at the Flying Fish in Carmel, I experienced a depth of love for myself that I had never felt from another person. This love was coming from within me, it was filling me up from the inside out. I only wanted Little Jana—the connection to her was what mattered most.

I closed my eyes and felt her, my Wise Little One was no longer across from me; she had returned to her place within me. Wholly content, I relaxed and enjoyed my Pinot Noir and the delicious meal, then paid the bill and left the restaurant. Heart connected, Little Jana and I walked down Ocean Avenue to the shore. The sun was setting over Pebble Beach, and the moon was rising in the east. As I stood on the beach, soaking up the beauty of the orange ball of fire descending over the horizon, I took a deep breath and knew I was all I needed. I kicked off my shoes and dug my feet into the cool sand. Little Jana rested. She was calm. She was fulfilled.

Back at the Inn, I sat on my balcony overlooking Monterey Bay. I balanced my computer on my lap and began to search for flights home to Santa Fe. There were a few options to choose from for my layover. I could stop in Salt Lake City, Phoenix, or Las Vegas. Vegas was an obvious choice—*great people-watching*, I thought, and the fact I was conceived there had always connected me to Vegas. Little did I know how much more the next day would hold for me.

I woke up the next morning, September 24, 2015, stretched, then stepped out onto the balcony at sunrise. Warm yellow and orange hues rose over Monterey Bay. A large cruise ship slowed as it approached the harbor. I closed my eyes, inhaling deep gratitude. I felt a renewed relationship to Little Jana—to myself. I felt something different in the air; something magical.

9/24/15 – Jonathan Livingston
Seagull – *my messenger*

I packed my bags, checked out, and headed to my rental car. As I loaded the trunk with my bags, a seagull flew over and perched on the railing of the parking garage directly in front of my car. My heart began to race with excitement. The seagull represented something profoundly special to me. As a young, single mother in Florida, I took up yoga. At the first class I attended, during savasana, the teacher read from the book *Jonathan Livingston Seagull*. It was a parable about a seagull who was never content with the status quo and decided to use his wings in a more purposeful way. He wanted to do more than hover above just the shore, scavenging for food to survive. Jonathan was intent on learning, growing, and soaring high with his God-given wings. As I stood in awe, a thought came and I asked out-loud to the gull, "Am I getting ready to go to my next level, Jonathan?"

I grabbed my phone and quickly took a picture of my spiritual messenger. I settled into the driver's seat feeling revitalized. A deep sense of knowingness had taken root in my soul. My body welcomed this feeling of exhilaration as I drove. Smiling wide, listening to music with the windows down, I reflected on all my Wise Little One had shown me about my life. I basked in the feeling of self-love and acknowledgment.

As I drove over the Santa Cruz Mountain, I soaked in the beauty. I took a satisfying breath and let it out audibly. My mind was flooded with images of my early years, and all the times I felt like I didn't want to live. I now looked at those experiences through a different lens—through Little Jana's eyes. I had been abandoning myself since I had been in the womb. The emotional connection between baby and mother is so intense that everything she feels comes to the fetus in the same way food does, through the umbilical cord. I felt the chronic tension and my mom's severe depression. It was during a hypnotherapy session that I discovered, in the womb, I tried to end my own life with the very cord that *gave* me life. The world seemed like a place that was relentless and cruel, filled with pain and grief. It didn't feel safe. Yet, I now knew that the world could be safe. It could be magical. I would continue to help Little Jana see this. I would offer her the love and support she didn't often receive, but absolutely deserved. Right there, behind the wheel of my rental car, I re-committed myself to putting my feelings first.

Getting closer to the city limits of San Jose, the traffic picked up. As I trained my eyes on the road, I reminded Little Jana that I would always listen to her and advocate for her highest good. I assured her that she could trust me to be the healthy parent she didn't have growing up. Together, we would relish in what was to come.

The foundational skill of emotional intelligence is self-aware-ness. Meditation is the spiritual tool we use to heighten our awareness of Self. When you're aware, you can manage your emotions which is the second skill of emotional intelligence. One way of managing emotions is the practice of reparenting; treating emotion like a loving parent would respond to their child. The next time you feel an uncomfortable feeling like anxiety, consider responding to it lovingly like you would an anxious child under the age of seven. Learning to reparent yourself is one of the greatest gifts you can give yourself.

*Chapter 02*

---

# WOMB

## 1965

*Flashes of soft light filter through my closed lids.*

*I feel the pull of the wide expanse of the Universe, yet I am here.*

*I am no longer infinite, softly cradled, and made of stardust.*

*I am tethered.*

*I feel something at my sides.*

*I lift them and inspect the ends, putting one in my mouth to explore its texture.*

*I feel two more things beneath me.*

*I rub them together.*

*I let myself feel comfort within the warm, soft cocoon.*

*Voices rise and fall on the outside.*

*I feel scared.*

*The voices get louder.*

*I am bumped.*

*I am slammed.*

*I hear muffled yells—one loud and shrill, one deep and purposeful.*

*I am bumped.*

*I am slammed.*

*I am shaken, then slammed again.*

*A scream.*

*Heavy, mournful wails.*

*My heart races alongside hers.*

I was in a place that felt unsafe.

With me always was a long, thick cord. As my body grew, the space around me seemed to shrink, creating a feeling of constant, nagging sadness. My eyes now open, my senses now heightened, I waited most days for the sharp, purposeful knocks to my body—the yelling, the sobbing, the flooding anguish.

On days when it was quiet, I felt empty—weak. I was not in a place where love permeated the walls. Instead, my body was flooded with feelings of sorrow. I no longer cared about learning about my surroundings, discovering my mobility, nor did I care to experience the world as I'd come to understand it. It seemed like a place that was relentless and cruel, filled with pain, grief, and unhappiness.

As days passed, I found myself succumbing to the panic and fear of the outside. I began to use the shrinking space to explore a way out—to escape before it was too late.

After what seemed like an unending amount of time, I found a way to get the cord around my neck, then I flipped, turned, rocked, and pulled, then seated myself in a way that felt stable. My base instincts called me to flip my head downward to prepare myself to enter the world, but I did the opposite, hoping instead to end the pain and suffering. I pulled the cord tighter. I steeled myself. I pulled tighter.

Then, the squeezing began.

The water around me drained.

I was being pushed out.

I began to grieve.

I had lost my will to live before my life on Earth officially began.

*Chapter 03*

---

# BIRTH
## ◦⌒◦ *December 21,1965* ◦⌒◦

The winter solstice. The shortest day of the year, and the darkest; an auspicious day to be born. One that marks the return of the light. When I eventually emerged from the womb, the umbilical cord was wrapped around my neck several times. I was blue and breach, curled into a ball with my fist squeezed shut. As they unwrapped the cord, jostled me, and slapped at my fresh skin trying to get me to breathe, the room was still and silent. My mom clenched her eyes. She stifled a sob. Then she cried out, "What's going on?"

More silence.

"Please, oh God, please," Mom whispered.

I wailed.

Mom let out a sob. "Oh God, thank you, thank you!"

The nurses lifted me up and wrapped me in a pink blanket. They put a blue and pink striped hat on my head, dabbed my face clean, then handed me over to my mom. I recognized her energy as soon as my flesh touched hers. She was happy, but she was also heartbroken in ways that only I understood—because I knew her from the inside. I'd heard her heart beating as it pumped my blood too. I felt it racing. I felt it slowing. I felt her pain. I felt *her.*

She held me in her arms and leaned over, staring me in the eyes. Her lips touched my forehead. Her cheek rested against mine. She whispered, "Welcome to the world, my precious baby girl."

I felt her love.

I *was* her love.

Mom and I stayed in the hospital for three days, then, when we were discharged, Granny brought us home. Although my mom and dad were still together, he'd made himself scarce during my birth and stayed far away after we got home. With postpartum depression on top of her chronic depressed state, Mom could barely function. She would sleep most of the day, as I would lay in the bassinet wailing from hunger. My cloth diaper wet; my skin inflamed with an angry rash. Mom's nipples were retracted so she was unable to get me to latch; breastfeeding was not an option. She had run out of baby formula and with no telephone, she'd have to wait until someone came to check in on her. Finally on my third day at home with little fluid and nutrition, my granny came.

Mom rested on the couch, as my granny sanitized the bottles and prepared the formula. My brother Roy toddled over and snuggled next to Mom and reached his chubby two-year-old arms out. Mom placed a pillow beneath his arms. She shifted in her seat. She placed me in his arms.

"Cradle her head. Be gentle," she said.

Roy looked down at me, elated to be a big brother. He kissed my head over and over. He pulled his arm out from beneath my legs and picked up my hand. He held it. "So tiny," he said.

"I know," Mom replied. "She is tiny. And you need to be a good big brother. You'll protect her, right?"

He nodded. "Yes, Mommy."

*Always.*

*Chapter 04*

# WHERE I COME FROM

## 1955

A s a child, my mom spent most of her time in trees, her 'pet' squirrel, Cleo, skittering across her shoulders onto the branches and rustling through the leaves. She had found the squirrel abandoned as a baby and bottle fed it until it was strong. Mom loved Cleo, she always talked about the day it disappeared. She was heartbroken to lose her little friend. She had saved its life, and it was bonded to her, but it was a feral animal, and its nature was to be free. If she wasn't climbing trees, she was down the street playing catch with the neighborhood boys. When the stars began to sparkle in the dusty pink sky, she'd head home to her safe place, tucked into life with her mom and dad.

My granny, Pearl Montgomery Haney, was only eighteen when she married my granddad. He was twenty years older than her; she married him to escape her father. My great-grandmother died when Granny was only eight; she was the second youngest of two brothers and nine sisters. Her father, my great granddad, began sexually abusing the younger daughters after their mother passed. Getting married and moving out saved Granny from being her father's victim.

One day in early May, when my mom was just twelve years-old, she was enjoying a typical day swaying in the branches with Cleo. That morning, her daddy had asked her to make him a special ham sandwich; one she'd perfected just for him. As lunchtime approached, Mom excitedly hopped down from the tree, banged through the screen door, and put Cleo in the cage. She put a plate on the kitchen counter and pulled two thick slices of pillowy Wonder Bread from the bag. She slathered the bread with mayonnaise, then piled it high with salty ham and juicy tomatoes. When she finished the sandwich, she asked her mom—my granny—where her daddy was.

"He's taking a nap," she said.

Mom left the kitchen, tiptoed down the hallway, and stopped at her parents' bedroom door. She knocked softly as she pushed it open and called out, "Daddy, your sandwich is ready."

*Silence*

She walked to his bedside, reached out, and tapped him. "Daddy?"

*Silence*

"Daddy?"

*Stillness*

"Momma! Momma! Please, Momma, help!" she called, panic rising in her chest.

Granny came running into the room, pushed Mom aside, took one look and yelled, "Call Aunt Verla!"

Hands shaking, Mom picked up the phone and asked to be connected to Verla who was there within moments with Mom's cousin, Judy, by her side. Mom was no longer allowed in the room but listened closely as Granny and Verla called for more help. Mom's daddy was dead from a massive heart attack, and she had found his lifeless body.

Mom and Judy sat outside on the front steps, Judy's arm around Mom who held her head in her hands. Through sobs, Mom repeated, "If only I had come in sooner to make his sandwich."

Yet the sandwich sat on the counter, untouched.

Mom was forever changed by that day and the loss of her daddy. Prior to his death, Mom had flourished under his loving adoration. She was the apple of his eye; he would pull up in his new '55 Chevy with gifts from his business trips. On one occasion, he brought home an RCA color television; they were the first family in the neighborhood to have one. Mom's dad showered her with attention and shielded her from the darkness in the world. Without her daddy, those feelings of being unconditionally loved were replaced with something hollow. She was left feeling lost and alone.

"Momma, please don't leave me." Mom begged as Granny began the nightly ritual of teasing her hair, applying blue shadow across her lids, and painting her lips deep magenta.

"Janice, you must accept your Daddy is gone, Honey. I will never meet anyone if I stay in this house every day and night."

The abandonment my mom felt increased as Granny stayed out late most nights, dancing salsa in Ybor City. This historic and legendary town near Tampa is filled with huge, old cigar factory buildings on cobblestone streets. Most of the factory workers were from Cuba, so the culture was infused with Latin food and dance. Granny began dating Latin men and wasn't providing Mom with the nurturing she needed.

Mom was the youngest of her two siblings, my Uncle Buddy, and Aunt Ginny, who were already grown and out of the house when their dad passed.

When we don't have emotionally intelligent parents to help us navigate the painful experiences like grief and heartbreak, we internalize the pain and personalize it. We make it mean something about us. Mom looked at the story of her daddy's death and made it mean she had done something wrong—that she was responsible for his death. She clung to that narrative. It became her truth.

*If only I had gone inside to make his sandwich sooner.*

This was the birth of one of Mom's core false beliefs.

*I am a bad girl.*

Without the grief counseling she needed, these thoughts began to possess her. Mom slipped deeper and deeper into her sorrow and soon found herself in a dark place. Within a few months, she stopped going to school. One time she left home for days on end, buying a Greyhound bus ticket, and traveling all over Florida with no intention of getting off the bus. She'd simply stare out the window and watch the landscape slide by. Panicked, Granny called the police who put out an all-points bulletin to search for her. She was eventually found and brought back home. Granny had reached her limit. She made the decision to send Mom to a girls' home for truancy in Tampa. There, Mom further imploded. She got her hands on a bottle of Aspirin and took every pill. They pumped her stomach, which saved her life. The problem was, Mom didn't believe she was worth saving.

This experience only created more alienation for my mom when she returned home. She never felt seen or heard by Granny. She never felt understood. She never felt supported. She often felt abandoned. The one and only constant in her life became her best friend from down the street: my dad—Archie.

My dad grew up in a house of never-ending turmoil. His father, whose family had immigrated from Ireland, was an alcoholic and had lost both of his legs working on the railroad. With chronic pain and phantom limb phenomenon, he turned to alcohol to calm his nerves. The alcohol slowly ate away at him and ravaged what was left of his body. My dad's mother—Big Momma—was a hard, severe Seminole woman who stood at 6'1". She was a towering force who wouldn't think twice about teaching a lesson with a swat of her hand or, far worse, hanging her husband out of the second-floor window without his prosthetic legs to show him who was boss.

In their house, chaos reigned supreme. My dad would come home from school only to find his parents embroiled in a violent, plate-shattering, wall-shaking fight. Like my mom, my dad was the youngest and the last of his three siblings left at home. Sometimes he'd walk inside and try to make it to his room without being caught in the swirl, but usually he didn't even bother. As he walked down the driveway, if he heard the familiar sounds of anger and violence, he'd turn on his heels and head down the street to his safe space. He'd sprint up the walkway and softly rap on the front door. The curtains of the window would flutter, and my mom would open the door and step outside.

Sometimes Mom and Dad would go for long walks, other times they'd head into town for an Orange Crush. One thing remained consistently true: their friendship provided the source of support and steadiness they both craved. With Mom, Dad got to be himself, showing a soft, tender side that most didn't get to see. He took pride in protecting Mom and comforting her when she felt the sharp sting of a life that got too hard too soon. Mom got from Dad much of what she lost when they lowered her father into the grave.

*A shoulder to cry on.*

*A hand to hold.*

*A heart to beat just for her.*

Most nights, Mom would wait for Dad outside, sitting on the front steps illuminated by the porchlight. She'd listen for the sound of him jogging up the street, sometimes with warm cookies he'd lifted from his kitchen. As the stars pulsed in the sky above, my parents would sit together eating the cookies, letting conversation carry them to safe spaces far away. Their knees would graze as they spoke. Their hands would brush. Sometimes they'd hold one another's gaze. But those moments always passed with a giggle from my mom, or a shake of the head from my dad. Theirs remained a strong friendship until they both turned seventeen.

On the night of the Spring Fling community dance, Mom teased and sprayed her hair to perfection. She then leaned into the mirror and finished her cat-like, pointed eyeliner and dabbed cherry-red lipstick on her small lips. She grabbed her purse and hurried out the door to find Dad waiting; his coal-black hair greased back, in black trousers and white t-shirt, the sleeves rolled with a pack of Winston cigarettes stuck on the left side. He walked right next to her all the way to the community center, helping her steady herself when her kitten heels caught on the dusty sidewalk.

The community center was buzzing. Dozens of teenagers sat on the stairs outside, smoking cigarettes and tapping their feet to the music that poured from the open doors. Mom and Dad dashed in, each found their group of friends, and hit the dance floor to move to songs by Chubby Checker, The Drifters, and, of course, Elvis.

As the fling was drawing to a close, Dad asked Mom to dance, and just as they started to move, a slow song began to play. For the first time, their bodies came together. My mom's hands rested on his shoulders. His hands sat in the perfect curve of her waist. As they swayed to "Are You Lonesome Tonight?", there was something about the way Dad's hands grazed Mom's hips that told her their friendship may be turning into something more.

That night, Dad walked Mom home to a chorus of crickets, urgently calling out to one another. They laughed as they made their way, recalling funny things their friends did and how ridiculous some of the new dance crazes were.

Their hands brushed once.

They brushed again.

Soon, they were intertwined.

Finally, outside of Mom's house, Dad pulled Mom into him. Instead of pulling back or looking away, Mom stared straight into his eyes. There they lingered in the bright streetlight, moths dancing in the sky above. Dad leaned in. Their lips met. They held one another and swayed, relaxing into the only thing in their lives that ever felt *right*.

## Chapter 05

# VEGAS

### ᚷᚥ *1963* ᚥᚷ

**T**here were only a handful of years between that first kiss and the day my parents, Janice and Archie Davis, became man and wife. There they were on the dance floor in the bright spotlight—the beauty queen and the top athlete, both achingly beautiful and full of big dreams. That night they clinked glasses of champagne, posed for the flashbulbs, and danced the night away. They couldn't have felt luckier, swept up in passion and romance.

*Mom & Dad's Wedding Day*

Once married, they said goodbye to their hometown of Plant City as quickly as they could. After all, they had all the trappings of a Hollywood couple, but they'd never have a chance to make their dreams of glitz and glamor come true, unless they left the small town behind. Dad with his slicked back hair, gawky frame, and sideways, flirty smile, was a dead-ringer for a singer who everyone was obsessed with at the time—Elvis. This fact was something they hung their hopes on as a newly married young couple. They made plans to move to Las Vegas where Dad could impersonate Elvis part-time while working in the casino, raking in tips as a blackjack dealer at the Golden Nugget.

For a while, in Vegas, things were wonderful. Dad's shows were packed, always drawing crowds of folks who would stay for pictures afterward, often handing Dad a healthy tip before leaving the venue. Mom would join him at after parties and at dinners at the casino. They made great friends and spent long, boozy nights in clubs and upscale bars with the new friends they'd gathered in Sin City.

Soon, however, Mom's belly began to swell—she was pregnant with my brother, Roy. And with that, her relationship with Dad began to change. Dad, like his family of origin, always had a fiery temper, which got worse when he drank. Mom, no longer interested in the party scene, spent her days at the public library. Her mindset was vastly different from Dad's and sharing all she was learning would cause my dad to explode.

*You think you're better than me?*

*Who do you think you are?*

*That baby will be a fucking bookworm like you are.*

Mom cradled her bump.

She whispered, *I'm sorry.*

After Roy was born, Mom and Dad's relationship quickly deteriorated. Dad continued to stay out drinking late into the night and would come home blacked out, often in a rage. He'd beat Mom as Roy screamed from his crib. Then, on the most explosive nights he'd walk out of the house and find himself another woman's bed to sleep in. On other nights, he'd pass out on the couch, leaving Mom to clean up after everything, calm herself, and soothe Roy while tending to her bruised and broken skin.

Emotional and physical abuse were wearing on Mom, but soon, things got even worse. Dad came home with big wads of cash, a mink wrap, jewelry and expensive bottles of bourbon and scotch. He'd give her gifts and watch her open them, her face contorted into a confused grimace as she asked, "But how can we afford—"

"It's fine, baby," he'd say. "The casino has just been really busy lately."

Nothing was adding up, and Mom was a smart woman. She soon figured out that he was skimming from the table, stealing from a place with known connections to the mob.

"Archie, you can't keep doing this," she begged. "They'll kill you."

"They'll have to catch me first," Dad said with a laugh. "I'm way ahead of them sonsofbitches."

Not two weeks after Mom figured out what he was doing, a group of men picked Dad up after a shift and drove him out into the desert. There, on the cold night sand, they beat him unconscious. Then they left him, bloody, bruised, and broken, assuming he was dead. Yet, he woke up, beaten so badly his eyes were swollen shut. He crawled, then he stood, then he began to shuffle his way to a main road to hitch a ride home.

At that point, Mom not only had Roy to take care of, but she was pregnant with me. She couldn't imagine continuing with Dad when he was always in trouble, bringing so much danger and destruction into her life and ours. So, clutching her belly with one hand and Roy's hand with the other, she climbed aboard a greyhound bus, headed for Atlanta where she had extended family.

She promised herself she was done with Dad.

But Dad always found a way to wiggle back in.

He begged.

He pleaded.

And he got it. . . *just one more chance.*

Their toxic cycle was set in motion.

Sometimes, having kids is enough to break a couple's toxic cycle. They take one look at the lives they have created and examine what needs to change. They vow to make those changes and they do it, life becoming more calm and joyful. For most couples, however, this is not the case; with kids, the dysfunction is amplified. The chaos is increased in its ferocity by kids screaming during arguments as they become more heated. Anger is heightened. Resolution rarely comes. Paradigms shift. Things feel. . . broken.

The Atlanta apartment was one where quiet was never something to relax into. Instead, quiet was a sign that something bad had happened or was about to happen. Every other time was chaos.

When I was just eighteen months old, Mom brought Roy and me down to the pool in our apartment complex. It was summer of '67 in Atlanta, hot and sticky, perfect for splashing the day away. Women in navel-revealing two-pieces surrounded the deck sipping from bright red cans of Coca-Cola as kids did cannonballs into the pool. A nearby radio played The Monkeys as Mom, in her oversized sunglasses and large, floppy hat, settled into a lounge chair with a magazine. Every time she flipped a page, she'd glance over at Roy and me, making sure we were okay.

Unable to be in the pool without an adult, I sat on the edge of the pool, my knees tucked into my chest. I stared into the water as it rippled, shifting between sparkling shades of white and blue. I found myself mesmerized, feeling a pull I can't explain. I wanted to tumble. I wanted to fly.

Mom happened to glance up when I shifted my weight and tumbled forward. My body plunged into the water, and I was instantly caught in a swirl of bubbles, which emerged around me like stars in the night sky. I rested for a moment at the bottom of the pool, listening to the echoes of panicked screams. Yet, before I could draw water deep into my lungs, I was grabbed by Mom and yanked. Together, we shot to the surface, sending fat drops of water cascading onto the pool deck. Mom sat me on her lap and patted my back while calling my name.

*"Jana Lee!"*

*"JANA LEE!"*

"What happened, Roy?" Mom shouted. She had expected him to watch over me. Roy was only four years old, and he began to cry. It was too much responsibility for him.

I sputtered and coughed, my lungs burning as I spit the water out. I blinked hard. I stared Mom in the eyes. I yearned to feel relief. I yearned to feel happy. I yearned to feel boundless love for the life I'd been given. Yet, I felt nothing.

When two dependent people get together, they create a co-dependent relationship. Co-dependency exists anytime an adult hands over responsibility for their feelings, their 'inner-child' to another. Co-dependency requires two dysfunctional roles, the 'taker' and the 'caretaker.' Takers believe others are responsible for their feelings. Caretakers believe they are responsible for others feelings. We can operate from both roles; however, we primarily default to one. Anytime you hear yourself or another say, "you made me feel" consider what role you most often are operating from. For example, the taker says, "you made me feel" and the caretaker takes responsibility for their feelings even if they didn't intend to hurt them.

## Chapter 06

# DADDY

### 1969

"Daddy, will you sing me a song?"

I toddled up to his lawn chair with my arms raised. He lifted his eyebrows, put down his beer, smiled and said, "Up ya go, my little Time Scalipuccini." I loved when he called me by this sweet pet name.

He pulled me onto his lap. I rested my head on his chest and he began to sing,

*Your time hasn't come yet baby*
*You got a lot of dreams to go*
*Your time hasn't come yet baby*
*But when it does your heart will know*

*You're gonna be a beautiful woman*
*Because you're such a beautiful child*
*And when you start to bloom*
*Just like a rose in June*
*I bet the schoolboys all go wild, but right now*

*Your time hasn't come yet baby*
*You got a few dreams to go*
*Your time hasn't come yet baby*
*When it does your heart will know*[3]

I closed my eyes and let myself drift. This was a special place meant only for me. I let myself listen to the percussion of his heartbeat, sink into the song, and enjoy this version of him before it slipped through my tiny fingers.

Although nights were often sleepless for Roy and me as we listened to voices rise and fall, we'd wake to something seemingly more stable. Mom would make breakfast, blaming bumps and bruises on late night falls, and Dad would either sleep late into the day or head out, returning sometimes several days later.

At times, I felt joyful and free with my daddy. He would swoop me up into his arms and dote on me, lovingly sweeping the hair out of my face, calling me pet names, and kissing my cheeks. I let his love fill me up. I let his attention satiate me. Yet, somewhere within, I sensed that I was not completely safe around him. At first it started as little warning flutters in my belly, but it soon developed into more obvious signs of anxiety. My heart would race, my palms would sweat, and my body would scream *NO!* anytime I'd get too close to him. Yet, I often had little choice. He would demand that I hug or kiss him, and when I resisted, he'd say, "Poor ole poppa, nobody loves me."

I'd look into his sad eyes.

I'd shift my weight between my feet.

I'd go to him.

With each forced hug and kiss, I was being conditioned to put his feel-

---

3 Elvis Presley, "Your Time Hasn't Come Yet Baby", Speedway (1968)

ings above my own. When he wanted his precious *Time*, I had no choice in the matter. He'd take me on his routes to deliver Lays Potato Chips, or my least favorite, when he wanted to go out for drinks but couldn't afford to pay for beer.

On days like these, Daddy would insist that I wear the pair of white ruffled panties he bought me. We'd go to a local dive bar filled to the brim with old slimy men, their skin and breath seeping with the smell of alcohol and Aqua-Velva. He'd then place me on the table and put upbeat music on the jukebox, then prompt me to dance. As men started to gather, he'd give me the signal to lift my dress and shake my booty to show off the panties. Men would hoot and holler and throw dollar bills and coins my way. Daddy would take the money and buy himself several beers before taking me to another place to do it all over again. As he drank, he'd prop me on a stool next to him and tell me how adorable I was. He'd push my hair behind my ears and smile before swigging his beer.

"My little girl."

I knew when he looked at me all he saw was my blond hair and my big, brown eyes. He never saw my innocence. My looks were something that softened him and allowed him to offer me his skewed version of love. I learned how to use that to my advantage. I knew how to bat my eyes, tilt my head, and pronounce my words in a cute, clumsy, way to manipulate him. That attention felt like love. But it also felt wrong. I was being conditioned to see my value through the lens of my looks. If I was pretty, then I was worthy and desirable. He exploited me and I was learning to exploit myself.

That feeling of his love being wrong didn't come all at once. It started slowly, then it grew roots, took hold, and spread into a gnarly feeling in my guts, that I couldn't ignore. Being around Dad began to feel more than uncomfortable—it felt scary.

*It felt dark.*

*It felt stifling.*

*It felt bad.*

As these feelings increased, I did everything in my power to distance myself from my dad. I knew the days of the week and times when he'd likely want me to go places with him and I'd curl up under my covers feigning sickness or hide under my bed or in a closet so he couldn't find me and take me along. Yet, I wasn't always successful.

One sweltering day, he came out of the house while I was splashing away in my plastic pool with my neighbor. He walked over and swept me into his arms and carried me to his truck.

"Take a ride with me, *Time!*"

"No, I don't want to go!" I shouted, "I want to stay and play!" But he didn't listen. He never listened.

My mom stood in the doorway with a concerned look on her face as she waved goodbye to us. He opened the driver's side door of his beat up, old, red Ford pickup, that had a rag shoved into the gas cap. He pushed me onto the long bench seat. He got in beside me and put his arm around me before slamming the door.

I swallowed hard.

"Now, stay close to me," he said with a smile. "Don't forget the other door is broken. I don't need you flyin' outta here onto the road."

He lit a cigarette then turned the key and the truck rumbled to life. My stomach tightened as we pulled out of the driveway and began heading down our street. He reeked of Old Spice aftershave, cigarettes and sour beer. His energy was too intense for me to handle. I cautiously inched away from him when he shifted gears so he wouldn't notice.

"Jana Lee, y'need to sit still now. Just stay right here next to me," he bellowed.

I shifted farther.

Farther still.

Soon, I was pressed up against the passenger's side door.

"I told you—" he began as the passenger side door flew open, and I fell out of the truck and rolled onto the street below. Dust swirled around me as I tumbled, the pavement scraping my knees and elbows. I rolled a couple of times, grinding dirt and gravel into my skin. Luckily, he'd been driving slowly, so I didn't land too hard. After screeching to a stop, he placed the truck in park and flew out of his door. My body ached and my skin burned, but my plan worked, my dad would have to take me home now. He picked me up and cried out, "Hot damnit! I told ya to stay next to me." He ran his hands over my hair and hugged me tight. "You're all banged up, my beautiful girl! What we gonna do with you now?"

"I want Mommy." I cried.

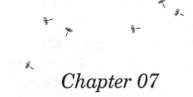

*Chapter 07*

---

# HOPE IS A BEGGAR

## ⌒ *1969* ⌒

*"Not hope, but faith. I don't believe in hope. Hope is a beggar.*
*Hope walks through the fire. Faith leaps over it."* [4]

—Jim Carey

As the years passed, my dad's patterns became very clear. The drinking would start slowly, just beer at first. After a while, he couldn't drink enough beer to get drunk, so he'd switch to whiskey. Once the hard liquor came into the picture, things changed quickly. His happy, carefree demeanor began to melt. He'd begin to slur his words, then his eyes would narrow, and his jaw would clench. He'd watch Mom as she moved around the house, seemingly waiting. Then he'd strike,

*What the fuck is wrong with you?*

*Get back in the kitchen before my dinner burns.*

*What's this pile of books here? What a waste of your life.*

There were more insults slurred, wrists grabbed, hair yanked, and slaps

---

4 Jim Carrey, Maharishi University Commencement Speech (2014)

across the face. Mom would oscillate between apologizing profusely and fighting back. But she was wearing thin, tired of all the hoping and wishing. All my mom wanted was love. That butterfly-inducing, knee-weakening kind of love—the kind they shared on late night walks beneath the moon when they were just kids. Yet, my dad wasn't equipped to love that way. He only knew how to love in the way his parents modeled. He loved conditionally; he loved harshly. Sometimes he didn't love at all.

Ever hopeful, Mom felt they had the best chance of finding happiness for our little family, was to return as a unit to Plant City. There, surrounded by old friends and family, they'd recapture what once was and maybe, just maybe, they'd be able to raise Roy and me *right*.

I was just four years old when our rickety, wood-paneled station wagon in desperate need of a new muffler, rumbled its way back into Plant City. The rural town sits between Orlando and Tampa in the center of the state. A typical small bible-belt southern town.

Ichepucksassa was the original name of the city. It was named after an Indian village that once occupied the area. People had such a hard time pronouncing the name, it was changed to honor Henry Plant, the railroad developer who brought the South Florida railroad through the state.

I pressed my nose against the glass and stared, wild-eyed at all the little town had to offer. Plant City is known for one thing outside of Florida, and that's the ability to grow strawberries straight through the year. This means that many strawberries sold in major grocery chains across the country come from Plant City, especially in the winter months. The small, sleepy town was so proud of this fact, they celebrated it by infusing everything with the sweetness of red berries. Annually in March, the town hosts the Strawberry Festival; some of the biggest country music stars come to perform. During festival time you can taste some of the finest shortcake, pies, and cobblers made from the freshest strawberries in the land.

"Look, Roy, look!" I called, tapping my finger on the glass, "It's a huge strawberry, LOOK!"

"Yep, that's the water tower," Dad called out over the sound of the Elvis 8-track crackling through the worn-out speakers.

"Whoa!" I said, straining to keep it in my line of sight as long as I could. I imagined the sensation of biting into it and it bursting in my mouth, sending sweet, bright red juice running down my chin.

As we rounded the corner, we pulled onto Main Street, which was buzzing with people. There were several small stores and gift shops, all advertising their own special strawberry treats. There was a soda shop, a pharmacy that sold root-beer floats and dozens of other businesses.

The red brick streets in the center of town eventually gave way to regular paved roads, lined with houses with wide wrap-around porches. In just a few turns, we arrived at our new house—it sat on the corner of Pennsylvania and Calhoun, just one block from where Mom and Dad grew up.

When we pulled into the driveway, Roy and I jumped out of the car, ready to stretch our legs. We ran across the yard before stopping to look back at the house. It was a white A-frame home with a small front porch and several windows facing the street. The front of the house was flanked with short, full palms, which added a feeling of privacy to the home. Just in front of the house stood an old, towering oak tree, which swayed in the breeze. Eventually, Roy and I held hands and made our way inside, wandering the small space, getting to know all its little nooks and crannies.

Having lived in Atlanta far away from family, I enjoyed a delicious feeling of comfort as the house filled with people on that first night. There was my granny, my aunts, uncles, and cousins, and my parents' old friends. First, they helped us lug all our belongings into the house and got us set up to live comfortably while we unpacked our things. Soon, the beer started flowing. The kids ran in and out of the house, playing games of tag or pretending to be spies, watching the grownups drink and smoke, their conversations collapsing into laughter every so often. Eventually, Roy and I fell asleep in the twin beds in our new room, lulled by the sounds of excited chatter. That's when I felt it.

*Hope.*

I came to understand later in life that *"hope is a beggar."*

I learned to replace hope with faith. Hope is wishing for something with attachment to the outcome. The energy of hope is weak. Faith, is detached and empowering, trusting that the Creator's will is greater than my own.

Some might have experienced life in Plant City as living a sweet slice of Americana every day. Roy and I would wake to the rattling sounds of the milkman coming to drop off fresh dairy. We'd then roll out of bed, fill bowls with sugary cereal and eat them in the living room in front of our little TV. Then, we'd head outside and play together across the street in Gilhrist Park, allowing ourselves to fall into a routine that felt *normal*. The neighborhood was full of kids who played outside until the streetlights came on, or the mosquito trucks chased them away with clouds of poisonous gas. Roy and I tended to stick together and played on our own most days. We'd tumble into games of pretend, always creating elaborate scenarios that took us far, far away. I'd be a princess and he'd be a knight—we'd slay dragons then retreat to our castle where we'd feast on cookies, cakes, and savory meats. Our reality was: when we looked in the refrigerator and cupboards, we didn't find much.

Our little house on the corner of Pennsylvania Street could have been home to so many sweet dreams—life's little miracles stacked one on top of the other until they touched the sky. However, wherever we were, chaos followed; always lurking ready to strike. Our family was impervious to happiness that lasted more than a few days at a time. We were trapped in a swirl of big emotions that ebbed and flowed. To look at our faces then, we were the picture of misery, in stark contrast to the happy little town we called home.

Each family of origin has a happiness setpoint. Our family's happiness setpoint was low. My parents recreated the same chaos that was pervasive in their childhood homes. Dad drinking and fighting and Mom victimized and abandoned. Our lives were black and white; our light was dim. Still, I had yet to see the violence between Mom and Dad. As soon as the fighting started, Roy would grab my hand and we'd scramble to our room together, or we'd burst through the front door, run to the side of the house, and play. We tried our best not to listen. We'd push ourselves to run and laugh or walk to the far edge of the yard and look at the big, historic homes with large verandas just down the block, imagining what was happening inside each one.

Eventually, Dad would stomp through the door and jump into his old truck, speeding off like a bat outta hell. The house would be silent except for soft sobs. That's when Roy and I would come out of our hiding spots or come back into the house and survey the damage. There would be shattered plates, toppled cups, and food flung on the floor. Mom would either be curled in a ball on the wood floor, or she'd be on the couch crying on the phone, sobbing to her sister, Ginny. Roy would sit next to her and put his arms around her while I wrapped my little fingers around the handle of a broom and began to clumsily sweep up the mess. I'd only stop to pull a chair over to the refrigerator and clamber up, standing on tiptoe until I could reach the freezer. I'd push my arm in as far in as I could, seeking something cool to calm Mom's wounds. Then, I'd go back to cleaning. After all, if I could put everything back in its place, wipe up the mess, and make order out of the disorder, I might be able to fix it all.

When things calmed down, I'd go outside and sit beneath a tree feeling the stability of its roots deep into the Earth. I'd close my eyes as the breeze caught the leaves, wrapping me in the soft pattering sounds as they fluttered. Praying to be saved from the constant fear and worry. I'd call out to God and beg for help. I begged, I pleaded, and eventually I raised my arms to the sky, mimicking what I had seen the adults do in church, desperately trying to get closer to Heaven.

*Please.*

*Save me. Please.*

## Chapter 08

---

# PILLOW

∽ *1970* ∾

I t was late at night, and I was having trouble sleeping. I rolled toward the wall, then back again, and back once more—my bed felt hard and unwelcoming, refusing to hold me softly. I wished Roy was awake to play games with me, but he'd been sleeping soundly for what seemed like hours. Frustrated, I rolled onto my back. The tree outside our window billowed in the wind, casting long, haunting shadows on the ceiling. The more I stared at them, the more certain I was I could pick out features. One eye. Two eyes. A long, pointy nose. Razor sharp fangs. Bony fingers, reaching. I pulled my floral bedspread up to my chin and closed my eyes. That's when I heard it.

At first there were low voices speaking quickly, then they began to rise and fall. The sound muffled by the walls; I couldn't hear exactly what they were saying—just pieces.

*How dare you.*

*Who the fuck do you think you are?*

*You bitch. . .*

Then there was silence.

Still scared of the bloodthirsty monster reaching its way across the ceiling, I rubbed my eyes and swung my feet onto the creaky wood floor. I slowly walked through the door and down the dimly lit hallway toward the living room. My nightgown grazed my ankles as I turned the corner. I stopped and stared, slowly processing what I was seeing. "Daddy," I whimpered. "What are you doing?"

His eyes were glazed over, he seemed possessed with something sinister, he was straddling my mom on the couch, holding a pillow over her face. Her legs were kicking wildly, her arms pinned to her side beneath my dad's knees. Locking eyes with me, he released his hands from the pillow. My mom bolted straight up. She gasped for air.

"What are you doing?" I repeated.

Dad slid off Mom without a word. He grabbed his bottle of Canadian Mist from the side table, staggered toward the door, lit a Winston, and lunged outside.

As the door slammed, I ran to Mom's side. She pulled me into her chest, holding my head against her large breasts. Her heart was racing, her breath was quick as she ran her hands over my hair. I pulled back and looked up at her, the tears in her eyes catching the sliver of streetlight that streamed through an opening in the curtains. She closed her eyes. She pulled me in closer and whispered, "Honey, you saved my life."

## *Chapter 09*

# GRANNY

## 〜 *1971* 〜

"It's Shake and Bake, and I helped!" I laughed, mimicking the little girl's sunny voice in the commercial. I was standing on a stepstool in Granny's house, dredging pieces of chicken in buttermilk, and then placing them one-by-one in a plastic bag filled with seasoned flour.

Granny stood behind me, her apron grazing the back of my head as she helped me grasp the bag.

"Okay, the oil should be ready now," she said, her mouth turned into a wide smile. My eyes glistened. I loved her happy, sweet wrinkles. "Time for you to step back and watch."

"Yes, Ma'am" I chirped.

I stepped off the stool and walked over to the stove, standing far enough away that splatters of oil wouldn't snap at my skin. I watched as Granny took pieces of chicken from the bag, one-by-one, tapped off the excess flour, and placed them in the crackling oil. She'd fry each piece until it was golden brown, and once the plate was piled high with chicken, she'd shake salt over the top. The smell of the crispy chicken cooking made my tummy growl and my mouth water. She'd serve homemade mashed potatoes with fresh cream and green beans from her garden. Then, she'd invite Roy and me to sit and eat with her. Our plates overflowing, we'd beg her to tell us stories, which she happily did, about the grandpa we never knew. We'd place our napkins in our laps and chew with our mouths closed, carefully showing the manners she was so lovingly teaching us.

As we ate, Mom came into the kitchen smoking a Virginia Slim. Her long hair was tucked behind her ears and draped down her back as she opened the refrigerator and reached for the pitcher of fresh brewed sweet tea. She stood and ashed her cigarette in the sink before reaching for a glass.

"Mom, look! It's Shake and Bake!"

"*And she helped*," Granny finished.

"That's nice," Mom replied flatly.

She sipped the sweet tea as she gazed through the kitchen window, looking out over the yard. From her view, she could see Granny's small pond amidst the large cypress trees, just beyond the thick saw palmetto bushes. Behind the pond, a few hundred feet back was a busy truck stop. A few years earlier, Granny had sold five acres to the developer. It was always buzzing with long-haul truckers and road-trippers stopping to gas up.

Mom stared blankly, smoking her cigarette to the filter, then reaching for a box of Luden's cherry cough drops, which she always sucked on after smoking. She leaned against the counter.

"Mom, do you want some?" Roy called. "It's really good!"

Mom shook her head and returned to her bedroom. That was the last we'd see of her for the day. It had been that way since we'd left Pennsylvania Street and moved in with Granny just outside the city limits of Plant City across from the train tracks. Mom was absent—a complete shell of herself since she'd left Dad behind after he almost suffocated her. The sparkle in her eyes was gone, replaced by nothing at all. Previously she'd been energetic, scurrying around the house, cooking, tidying, doing everything she could to make things right. She'd sometimes sing along to records as she prepped meals, and even dance as she mixed and stirred.

At night when things were quiet, she'd devour books, licking her fingers before turning each page. I'd run up to her. She'd ruffle my hair. She'd kiss my forehead. She'd hold me close. Now she was cold, teary-eyed, and drained of the magic that made her my mom. But that's what major depression does. It creeps in like a hungry monster, taking up space in your being. It digs its claws into the walls of your mind, opens its hungry mouth, and consumes every piece of you—never satiated. It takes until there is nothing left. My mom had been devoured, and I desperately wanted her back.

I slowly opened my eyes and wiggled my toes. I was cozy, wrapped in a blanket beneath my little twin bed in Granny's house. I'd been dreaming that I was flying, soaring high above Plant City, ready to bite into the giant strawberry. As I crawled out from beneath the bed, I heard men's voices calling back and forth to one another.

*She's not here!*

*What about over there?*

*Nothing!*

*Could someone from the truck stop have grabbed her?*

*I'll run over there!*

*Guys, we're gonna need to drag this little pond.*

*Let's go, right now, we're wasting time!*

My mom stood near the pond, wailing.

"Jana Lee!?" She screamed, "Where are you!? JANA LEE!"

That's when I realized—they were looking for me.

Granny rubbed Mom's back as she lit cigarette after cigarette. I stared over the scene, fascinated. Mom had barely looked in my direction since we'd left the little house on Pennsylvania Street, and now she was bawling at the thought of me being gone. I restrained my urge to move as I stood motionless and looked out the screen door; something inside me smiled.

Instead of bolting out the door, straight into their arms, I quietly turned around and crawled back under the bed, pulling the blanket around my body. I wanted to let out a huge laugh—I was right there, but all these people thought I was *nowhere.*

I stayed under the bed for as long as I could, imagining how Mom would react when she saw me. She'd cry out in relief. She'd shower me with love. Maybe she'd even buy me a present?

After I listened to the panic for a long, long time, I threw off the blanket and slid on my belly out from beneath the bed. I made my eyes look extra sleepy as I crept toward the screened back door. The springs screeched as I pushed the door open. "Mommy?" I said, softly, pretending to rub sleep from my eyes.

"JANA LEE!" She shouted, dropping her cigarette, and running to me with Roy and Granny following closely behind. She scooped me up in her arms and held me tight. I let my body melt into hers as she sank to the ground, cradling me.

"Mommy, what's going on?" I asked. "Who are all these people?"

"They were all helping us look for you, you scared us half to death!"

"Where were you, baby?" Granny asked.

"I was asleep, under my bed. I'm sorry," I said, widening my eyes.

"It's okay, it's okay," Mom repeated. "I'm just so happy you're all right."

She held me close, rocking me back and forth, kissing my forehead over and over. She sang softy in my ear,

*You are my sunshine, my only sunshine*
*You make me happy when skies are grey*
*You'll never know dear, how much I love you*
*Please don't take my sunshine away*[5]

I took in her smell—Aqua Net and Ivory soap. This love—this soaring sort of love—is all I had ever wanted from a parent. As she lifted me and

---

5 Jimmie Davis and Charles Mitchell, "You Are My Sunshine" (1940)

carried me back into the house, I looked up into the tree branches as they bent in the hot breeze. She put her hand on the back of my head. She pushed her cheek against mine. I closed my eyes aware that if I wanted her love, I'd have to *earn it*, even if it meant pretending to be gone. Unknowingly, I was being conditioned to believe that to get her attention—even have my needs met—I needed to act out.

In the wake of my 'disappearance' Granny decided it was time for us to move even farther outside of town. The truck stop bordering the property caused too much fear that I might actually *be* snatched.

A month after the incident, a massive heavy hauler pulled into the driveway. Mom, Granny, Roy and I watched in amazement as the little A-frame house was lifted off its foundation and loaded onto the truck. By the end of that day, we were unpacking and moving back into our shared bedroom with Mom. Once we were settled, things with Mom began to change. Instead of spending her days in bed, only coming out occasionally for a drink or something to eat, she was now working at the Kash 'n' Karry grocery store in the bakery. She'd head to work every day in her uniform, then come home smelling like butter and sugar. The smell swooped me into a swirl of memories of delicious things she'd bake and watch me devour. For my seventh birthday, she made me the cake of my dreams. It was a Cinderella cake decorated with white frosting, little pink flowers, and a horse-drawn carriage—the most elaborate cake I'd ever seen. Being so close to Christmas, my birthday was typically overlooked. But not this year. The Cinderella cake was so perfect, so incredibly special to me that I didn't want to eat it. I had spent all day pretending to be the small Cinderella figurine in the carriage with my handsome Prince. It wasn't until later that evening that I shrugged my little shoulders, slowly nodded in agreement, and allowed Mom to cut the cake.

While working at the bakery, Mom met a man named Marvin who treated her like gold. He was a sweet, well-educated man five years her junior, who celebrated her intelligence instead of berating her for it. Above all else, he made her intensely happy. All of this meant that she still wasn't around much—but now it was for reasons that were good. She'd often bring cookies or cupcakes, which Roy and I would hold in two hands and munch while sitting on the porch next to sweating glasses of lemonade while Mom got ready for her nightly date with Marvin.

Granny had quit her job at Newkirk's barber shop to take care of Roy and me full-time. That's when my relationship with Granny went from close to even closer. For all my life up to the point when we moved in with Granny, I'd been praying to be saved from the conflict and chaos. Granny took such great care of us, teaching us life's lessons that we missed in the mayhem.

During this time, I began to act out sexually. Once, when I was six, Granny caught me under our house with a neighbor boy gyrating on me and shamed me for it. On another occasion, I discovered the jets at my aunt's in-ground pool felt good when I pressed my private parts on them. I was showing signs of being sexualized at a very young age, yet I didn't have any recollection of being molested or violated.

*Being around Dad felt more than uncomfortable—it felt scary.*
*It felt dark.*
*It felt stifling.*
*It felt bad.*
My Wise Little One was sounding an alarm.

I needed the stability my Granny provided. She recognized my fears and generalized worry and would do what she could to help. Those days were different—no one was addressing childhood trauma—issues like mine were simply downplayed or ignored. She'd hold me tight on days that were particularly bad, read me stories, and make me big, comforting meals. But simple actions like that wouldn't always do. Especially on days when outside circumstances made my anxiety more severe.

The year I turned seven, I had the opportunity to ride on the Kash 'n' Karry float in the Strawberry Festival Parade. That morning as Granny dressed me in my long strawberry gown with lace petticoat, which my Aunt Ginny had sewn for me, Granny noticed me shaking violently, taking short, shallow breaths. I wanted to curl into Granny's arms. I wanted to run.

I was panicking.

Unsure of what to do, Granny broke off a tiny piece of a Valium she had in her purse. Soon after I swallowed the pill, there was a problem. Although I could feel it calming me, it was making me horribly sick. As soon as the parade started, I began to vomit violently. Seeing my distress, Marvin grabbed a bucket and walked alongside the float for the entire route. I smiled and waved as much as I could, but every few minutes I was gagging and heaving.

During a lull in my queasiness, I looked around, noticing dozens of beautiful girls in full faces of makeup marching and waving merrily. They had perfect hair, store bought dresses, and big, pearly white smiles. Their moms and dads stood in the crowd together in coordinating outfits, beaming at their well-groomed daughters. Yet, there I was, in a homemade dress now flecked with vomit, barely able to catch my breath, with my mom's boyfriend wandering beside me with a bucket. As drums beat steadily and high school bands' music roared, I hung my head. It was the first moment in my life when I noticed a line that existed between me and other little girls my age. It created within me a deep, powerful hunger. I didn't want to be different. I wanted to be just like them. This was it: the birth of one of my core false beliefs.

*I'm not good enough.*

Plates clattered as my nose perked up at the smell of coffee and maple syrup. I stared at Granny as she perused the menu, although she knew it by heart. This was our tradition—a special time for *us girls*—breakfast at the famous Lani Purcell's Holiday Inn. I copied Granny, placing my napkin in my lap before lifting the menu to review it. Even though I always ordered the same thing, I liked looking over the names of all the sweet treats as I enjoyed the hustle and bustle of the restaurant.

Granny nodded to me when the waitress approached the table, signaling that I should order for myself.

"May I have buttermilk pancakes with a side of crispy bacon and fresh squeezed orange juice, please?"

"What a sweet girl you are," the waitress said with a smile. "And for you?" she asked, turning to Granny.

"I'll have the same," she said.

Granny sipped her coffee as the waitress walked away. "So," she asked, eyebrows raised, "do you want to talk about last week?"

I shook my head *no*.

Granny raised an eyebrow, and I smiled sheepishly back at her. I'd been getting in trouble a lot at home and school, and the most recent issue was a big one. Carolyn was my next-door neighbor. She would come over to play school with me, and I was always the teacher. I'd pace the front of the 'classroom' and ask questions, then motion for Carolyn to answer. Anytime she got the answer wrong, I'd smack her on her arm with the ruler. In my mind, this was what you did when someone said or did something wrong—it's what we did in our house. I'd seen this behavior modeled my whole, short life.

A few days before breakfast with Granny, I was walking along our country road with another neighbor friend, Tammy, laughing and talking about the day. Just then, Carolyn and her visiting cousins from Georgia came out from behind a row of trees and jumped on me all at once, pulling my hair out, punching me, and kicking me as hard as they could. Tammy took off fast as she could to get help, sending the girls running.

When my mom saw the three-inch bald spot on my head, she charged next door to Carolyn's house. She rushed up to the door and began to beat on it with her fist. From behind the door a woman's voice shouted, "get the hell out of here, you crazy bitch, I'm calling the police." Mom, eerily calm, turned back toward our house and walked into the kitchen grabbing a knife out of the drawer. Granny pleaded with Mom, "Janice, let's call the police, please don't do anything stupid." Mom didn't say a word, she turned and walked through the screen door, slamming it behind her. Granny, Tammy, and I huddled by the back window watching. Mom walked to the clothesline and began pinning clothes on the line, nonchalantly as if nothing had occurred. A few minutes later, Carolyn's aunt from Georgia, came creeping up behind Mom. I wanted to scream and alert her, but right at that moment, Mom turned pulling the knife out from her waistband and lunged towards the woman. The woman backed up, her face distorted in fear, and ran back to her house. My mom was becoming just like my dad.

Now, Granny wanted to talk to me about it.

"Are you sure?" she asked.

I nodded, reaching for my orange juice.

"Okay then," she sighed. "But we'll have to talk about it soon. For now, make sure to cross your legs like a lady, little miss. Remember, that's what we are: we are proper southern *ladies*."

I crossed my ankles beneath the table and straightened my posture. Granny smiled.

I felt my face flush and turn red hot with shame at the memory of acting out and being mean to Carolyn. The side of my head throbbed; evidence I too was just like dad. It was all I knew, fighting and chaos – at seven years old, my conditioning was nearly set. Mom would say, "You're just like your dad's sorry-ass side of the family," when she didn't like how I was behaving.

Soon, plates were placed in front of us. This was the best part—anticipating the first bite of fluffy buttermilk pancakes slathered with butter, swirled with maple syrup. I carefully picked up my knife and fork, looking at Granny for approval. She nodded as I carefully cut into the stack, slowly taking my first mouthful. I kept my mouth closed as I chewed, then reached for a piece of crisp, salty bacon.

Times like this with Granny represented calm in the chaos. The steady that balanced the quakes. She was one of the greatest gifts of my life. The precious moments like these allowed me to see glimpses of happiness amid the swirl of heartache and helplessness.

The very next week, Granny sat my mom down and told her that the incident with Carolyn and her cousins was the last straw. She never wanted to abandon Roy or me, and it wasn't even my acting out she was finished with. It was my mom, her reaction to what happened, and the way she handled everything in our lives. Granny had spent so much time caring for us all, making sure we felt safe and loved. But what she really wanted was to make up for the fact that after Mom's father had passed, she hadn't been there for her. Granny wanted nothing more than to make Mom feel whole again but had finally accepted that she couldn't help someone that didn't want to help themself. Mom had already bought into the false belief that she was bad, insignificant, and worthless, and she operated from that belief. She either folded into herself and disappeared when things got hard, or lashed out, kicking and screaming. It was a self-fulfilling prophecy. It was finally over with Granny. She couldn't take it anymore.

Even though Granny had said she was leaving because of my mom's behavior, I didn't believe her. I felt in my heart that I had pushed away the one and only stable, constant force of love in my life – further solidifying another false belief of mine.

*I'm unwanted.*

Once Granny moved across the state to the east coast in Ft. Pierce, Mom felt the only choice she had at that time was to marry Marvin. After all, it wasn't a bad choice. Marvin was a wonderful, loving man who genuinely cared for all of us. Not long after we waved goodbye to Granny, they were married at the courthouse. That's when Roy and I would be given a taste of the life we truly deserved.

*Chapter 10*

# FISH FARM
## 1971

**R**oy and I sat in the backseat as Marvin's little Renault sped along the winding back roads. Marvin looked over at Mom, smiled, shifted gears, and placed his hand on her knee. "I think we're going to be really happy here."

Mom gazed back at Marvin and smiled.

I smiled too.

However, I was aware of an ache; a feeling of emptiness I had come to know so well. I was hungry for my granny and her love. I closed my eyes and leaned my head against the window, my forehead hitting the glass with each bump. I let my imagination wander to her. *I am on her lap; she's scratching my back. I'm in bliss; held; mothered; protected; nurtured.* There wasn't anything my granny didn't give me. She spoke every one of my love languages. Without her, I began to feel unstable; like the world was unsafe.

Finally, the car rolled up the long driveway, causing my head to bump against the glass a little harder. I was jolted back. I gazed over the sandy flat landscape and big, billowing trees.

We pulled up in front of one of the two houses on the property and got out of the car. Mom stepped out first and walked over to the driver's side. Marvin got out and opened his arms. She kissed him on the cheek, turned, and leaned her back against his chest, staring over the wide expanse of land. Roy and I slid out of the car together, both bouncing in place. We looked over at Mom. "Please, can we?" I begged.

"Go ahead, you two," Mom said with a giggle. "Just don't go too far, you hear?"

Roy and I took off running, the soft drone of cicadas draping itself around us as we went. The un-mowed grass stung our ankles as we bolted, sending grasshoppers hopping out of the way. Soon, breathless, we began to walk, stopping to explore trees, small clearings, trying to catch butterflies along the way. Once we turned back, Marvin was carrying Mom over the threshold of the house, leaving Roy and me to enjoy the distinct feeling of freedom that came from running wild.

The property was a functioning tropical fish farm with two houses on it. The one we'd live in was a small house with two bedrooms, a sitting area, and a tiny kitchen. The only bathroom was an outhouse located on the back porch. The bigger house was two-stories and overlooked the entire property. Behind it were endless rows of trenches, home to thousands of tropical farmed fish. Roy and I walked as far as we could, only turning around when mosquitos began to devour our legs and beads of sweat began to roll down our faces.

On our way back to the house, we stopped beneath a gigantic, old oak tree to rest. I stared up into the swaying Spanish moss that draped over the thick branches. Roy picked up a stick and began swinging it, pretending he was fighting Godzilla in Tokyo.

I looked toward the house watching my mom and Marvin unpack the car. So much of me felt excitement—thrilled to be in this space where Roy and I could roam and play. Yet, inside me felt heavy, like a brick laying on my heart. The weight of sadness never left me. Even as the sun shone brightly in the sky, its rays begging us to come out and play, my little body didn't want to move. Instead, I wanted to do what I always did, retreat into myself and fold into a daydream.

As the weeks went on, Roy and I fell into our familiar pattern. We'd wake with the sun as it made its way through the curtains in our small, shared bedroom. We'd roll out of bed and into our raggedy clothes, then would burst through the screen door and bolt out into the fields. Our first stop was always our favorite tree—the big, old oak. We'd linger under that tree for a while, challenging one another to jump high enough to touch the tips of our fingers to the swaying Spanish moss. Then, we'd run to the far edge of the property where the trees were younger and easier to climb. We'd pull ourselves up onto the lowest branch and climb higher and higher until the branches became thin and brittle. Roy would climb behind me the whole way up, quickly placing his hand on my back if I slipped.

Once we climbed back down, we'd run across the field, past the two-story house and out toward the fish troughs. The water in the troughs was never still, always churning with the movement of the fish crowded inside. Roy and I would walk slowly along the troughs looking for frogs. When we locked eyes on one, one of us would pounce. We'd hold onto them for a bit, running our hands along their slimy backs and touching their webbed feet before letting them slide back into the water. Occasionally, we'd bring a bucket and see how many frogs we could catch. Once the bucket was full, we'd bring them to Mom, she'd cut the legs off, dredge them in flour, and fry them up for dinner along with grits and fried green 'maters'.

As the sun dipped lower in the sky, we'd make our way back to the house. Mom would have dinner cooking as Marvin returned home from a full day of classes at the University of South Florida. Marvin always greeted Mom with a kiss and Roy and me with a big hug. When we'd sit for dinner, Marvin would ask about our day and listen as we talked excitedly about the frogs and our best tree climbs. He nodded and smiled, asking questions about the adventures we had. He'd even ask Mom about the books she was reading or ask her opinion on things he had going on at work. I felt relaxed—I could taste my food, enjoy the moment, and be present without worry.

After dinner, Marvin would help Mom clean up as Roy and I did our homework. On bath nights, I'd climb into the tub on the screened-in back porch. The sun would sink below the horizon and fireflies danced as I soaked in the womb of the water until my fingers pruned. When I finished my bath, I'd get into my pajamas before curling up in bed, ready for stories read by Marvin and Mom. For a short time, it was peaceful and harmonious in the 'little house'.

Marvin and Mom's marriage did not mean the end of Mom's connection to Dad. He always seemed to be around, lurking on the periphery of our lives.

*Waiting.*

My soon-to-be cousin, Michelle, and I sat on the floor of my bedroom playing with my ratty, old Barbie dolls. Her mother, Gloriana, was about to marry Mom's brother, Uncle Buddy. I couldn't wait for the ceremony and for us to *officially* be family, especially since we'd grown so close. She was one of the only girls I spent time with, playing 'house' and pretend while our parents spent time together doing whatever grownups did.

"Oh Ken, I love you so much. Take me away from this place." She squealed, walking Barbie toward Ken.

"Yes, Barbie, I will rescue you, but first. . ." I rasped, banging Ken's face against Barbie's.

*Muah, muah, muah!*

That's when we heard it. My mom's voice shouting from across the lawn. We ran to the window and looked out and saw she and Gloriana standing face to face, Mom was screaming at her. Gloriana's eyes were wide, her face full of fear. She was paralyzed by Mom's rage.

*You whore!*

*You disgusting BITCH.*

She grabbed Gloriana by the hair and yanked her to the ground. Michelle and I held on to each other, pressed against the windowsill as the screaming continued.

*Archie? You SLEPT with my Archie?*

*You—*

Mom's fist rained down blows on Gloriana's head, screaming and punching her in the face. She was still clutching clumps of hair when my uncle pulled Mom off.

Breathless, Mom repeated, "Archie? You fucked Archie, you bitch?" Uncle Buddy didn't seem to be very rattled by the fight. He picked Gloriana up from the ground and carried her to the car shoving her inside.

Later that night as Mom iced her knuckles, Marvin sat across from her at the dining table while Roy and I listened, our ears pressed against the closed door to our bedroom. In hushed tones, Marvin talked, asking Mom how he could stay with her when she still had such intense feelings for Dad—so intense that she'd beat Gloriana like a rabid animal. Mom had no answers, and that was answer enough. That's when we said goodbye to the only constant, healthy male presence I'd ever known.

That day, devastated by what had happened, Marvin went to the Strawberry Patch bar and liquor store. There, sitting at the bar minding his business, some drunk picked a fight with him, busting a bottle on his head. In reaction, he stood from the barstool, went to his car, grabbed a club, and went back inside. He hit the man over the head with the club, killing him. Marvin was convicted of voluntary manslaughter. Six years in the state penitentiary changed Marvin. As soon as he was released, he began dealing drugs and hanging with a motorcycle gang in St. Petersburg. As I grew older, he would visit us periodically, bringing gifts and slipping Mom some cash. He always loved her. One evening when I was in my early twenties while visiting my granny, *America's Most Wanted* came on the TV. There plain as day, was a picture of Marvin, he was wanted for first-degree murder. This was the second time he had killed. This educated, sweet, kind man would now spend the rest of his life in prison. I wonder what would have happened to him had he never met my mom.

*Goodbye, Marvin.*

*Chapter 11*

---

# BACK TOGETHER
### ∽ *1972* ∾

*Learn the alchemy true human beings know.*
*The moment you accept what troubles you have been given,*
*the door will open.* [6]
—Rumi

Losing Marvin was painful—not just for me, but for Roy too. With Marvin in our lives, Roy and I had gotten a taste of what family life felt like without constant turmoil. We were free to live life as little kids, roaming free with few worries, only to return to a house that felt like *home*. Now, things were changing, reverting to something we knew all too well. With Marvin gone, my mom had fallen back into that well-known dark place, which was jarring after such a long period of relative peace and calm. Her energy was heavy, her mood unsteady. Soon, however, there was a break in the clouds.

"Jana Lee! Roy!" We heard Mom call from the front porch. "Get back here!"

---

6 Rumi, *The Essential Rumi*, ed. Coleman Barks (Harper Collins, 1995)

Roy and I dropped our frog buckets and ran through the field toward the house. As we jogged beneath our favorite trees, we jumped to touch the Spanish moss, letting it tickle our fingers. We arrived back at the house, breathless.

"Yes ma'am," we called in unison.

"Y'all won't believe it," Mom said with a smile. "Mr. Connor, the landlord is moving away, and he said we can move into the big house!"

"Really?" I squealed.

Roy let out a *yesssss* and punched the air excitedly.

"Yes! We'll move in as soon as he leaves, and it should be really soon."

I hugged Mom around the knees. She reached down and rubbed my back. I closed my eyes and smiled to myself. For the first time since Marvin left, I felt optimistic.

Over the next several weeks, the mood in the house lifted. Mom would turn up the stereo and sing, Johnny Nash's number one hit, "I Can See Clearly Now" as we excitedly packed our things into boxes and bags for the move across the yard. The first time we went into the house, Roy and I bounded over the threshold and ran from room to room, each claiming our spaces. For the first time ever, we would each have our own room. Mine was on the ground floor. It was small, with a big window looking out over the fish farm. On that first day, I closed the door and relished in the silence. I opened my most important bag of all— the one filled with Barbie dolls. Before I did anything else, I dumped the Barbies onto the floor of my bedroom and arranged them in a corner near the big window. There, I'd be able to sit and play in a fat beam of sunlight. The best part? Mr. Connor had left his cocker spaniel, Scottie who would lay in the sunspot with me, snoozing sweetly as I gave my Barbie's life. My room was my haven—my personal chambers in the castle we now called home.

Roy's bedroom was pure magic. It took up most of the entire upstairs along with a room for canning pickled vegetables and jams. His bedroom was surrounded by towering picture windows. You could see the entire farm from his vantage point—a perfect place for dreaming. On some nights, we'd climb through the window and crawl onto the roof where we'd lay side-by-side and stare at the stars until the mosquitos began to devour us. We'd talk about the meaning of life; we would share secrets and swap stories about school. Slowly, joy was returning to our lives. I suppose we should have anticipated what was to come. For us, that light, free feeling of happiness and stability was always temporary.

Not long after we moved into the two-story house, my mom let my dad come back. It had been nearly three years since Dad lived with us. He showed up in his beat-up truck filled to the brim with his things. He got out, his signature toothpick hanging from the corner of his crooked smile, hooked his thumbs in his belt loops, and surveyed the property. Mom skipped out of the house and ran toward him. He wrapped her in a tight hug, lifted her off the ground, kissed her, and put her down next to him. She put her arm around him. Dad locked eyes on Roy and me playing across the field. "*Time!*" he called out.

I found myself running toward him, even jumping into his arms, letting him swoop me into a tight hug.

"Time Scallapucini, how ya doin'?" he bellowed.

"Good!" I replied. He put me down. The foul smell of cigarette smoke lingered on my clothes.

Roy walked toward us slowly. Dad greeted him with a pat on the back and gave Mom another kiss and a slap on the butt. She swatted him on the shoulder and giggled.

"Ok, it's time for a tour!" Dad said with a laugh as he pulled a trash bag filled with clothes out of the back of the truck.

My belly ached as I watched him walk around the house with his cocky swagger, surveying the rooms. His energy was hard and weighty—almost dangerous. I tried to calm myself, but my internal alarm bells rang. He was my daddy. I loved him. But something about him always felt off. His presence was like a puzzle piece that just didn't fit. As much as Mom tried to push Dad into place, the shape of him was all wrong.

Though still nervous around Dad, I settled into his presence quickly. He and Mom seemed genuinely happy together, laughing, sharing sweet kisses, whispering secrets. I sometimes found myself smiling as I watched them together. They were Elvis and Priscilla, so passionately in love, their eyes were starry like the night sky. He was sweet and tender toward me, showering me with compliments and singing softly to me when I curled up beside him. Every evening when he came home from work, I'd run to his truck to see what treat he brought me that day. I'd dig into a bag of salty chips or fluffy, sticky Twinkies.

"Here, Scottie!" I'd say as I dropped a piece of my snack for him.

As sweet and gentle as Dad was to me, I hated the way he treated Roy, who was becoming increasingly anxious and withdrawn, for good reason. He was a tender, shy boy, and had turned to food to soothe his anxiety. He'd gained a considerable amount of weight and had to wear pants from the 'husky' section at the store. Before Dad came back, Roy was only lightly teased by Granny who had given him the nickname "Husky". Those seemingly innocent jabs created shame in my brother about his weight and Dad's return made things even worse. There were dozens of insults Dad would hurl, "Pansy-Ass, Sissy," but his favorite was, "Lard-ass," which he'd hiss in Roy's direction any time he was agitated. The more verbal abuse Roy endured, the shier and more reserved he became. It was as if Roy was a manifestation of Dad's self-loathing, he saw in Roy what he hated in himself – his tender side. Under the constant criticism, Roy's insecurities began to eclipse every other part of his personality. He over-compensated by acting as the class clown at school and putting on comedy shows for Mom and me at home when Dad wasn't around.

Feeling his hurt, I drew closer to Roy, trying to love the pain out of him by remaining a happy, playful force in his life. We would spend hours pretending to be contestants on *Let's Make a Deal* and *The Price is Right*. Roy would shout, "Jana Lee, you are the next contestant, come on down." I would squeal and run through our small living room back and forth, jumping with joy.

Mom and Dad eventually remarried in a private ceremony at Eastside Baptist church with Roy and me by their sides. They were both re-baptized, becoming born again Christians, vowing to live a clean life. As well as I knew my parents, I was still a naïve child, and believed this time could be different.

We left the ceremony that day as a family feeling connected for the first time that I could remember. Deeply ensconced in the church and its teachings, I had faith in Jesus and knew he would protect us as he made Mom and Dad new again. The honeymoon phase stretched on as they continued to express their love in big and small ways. As a family, we shared dinners together, went to barbecues with our aunts, uncles, and cousins, and spent lots of time at the new Pentecostal church they were attending. There, I would play my tambourine and sing to the top of my lungs, *"Jesus on the mainline, call him up and tell him what you want."* I would dance and jump up and down like the adults. In worship, I didn't just *believe* in Jesus, I felt Him. On one occasion, as I sang and played my tambourine, I felt something come over me. I dropped to my knees, then began to convulse on the floor, writhing and shaking. The Holy Spirit had gotten ahold of me. In that moment, on the floor of our church, I had my first mystical experience. It was as if my soul remembered I was a spiritual being having a human experience. I was free. I was safe. I was protected. I was loved. *I was love.* I was in ecstasy with God.

Just moments later, I returned to my body, my eyes blinking wildly as I got my bearings. Members of the church swept me up, celebrating my experience with shouts of praise. "Hallelujah" and "Praise the Lord" rang through the church. I let the experience linger in my heart for as long as

I could. That love—the Infinite kind—was what I desired most but could only manage to grasp for short bursts of time.

There is no 'right' form of Spiritual guidance. We have many names for our spiritual source of love and wisdom: the Divine, God, Spirit, Higher Power, Holy Spirit, Creator, The Universe to name a few. The truth is you are here for a reason. You are never alone  You are always being guided to your highest good. You are not separate from the Creator. You are a spark of the Divine encapsulated in a human body suit. As the French Jesuit priest, Teilhard de Chardin said, "You are a spiritual being having a human experience."

## Chapter 12

# CYCLES

⤳ *1972* ⤳

The state of my family began to feel tenuous, just like it always had before. Although still largely sweet toward one another, Mom and Dad were starting to bicker more frequently. Many times, it was over small things: dinner not cooked on time, the television too loud. Other times, it was about something bigger: Dad's lingering glance at another woman, the lack of money, Mom nagging Dad to communicate his feelings. I was starting to feel nervous all the time. Even as a young girl, I knew the truth. My parents had built a track that they'd traveled many, many times together in life. No matter how hard they tried to forge a new path, it seemed they were destined to return to the one forged in chaos and heartbreak. It was cyclical.

As fall brought slightly cooler temperatures, one Sunday afternoon, Mom invited Dad's family over for a barbeque. Big Momma rarely visited; she didn't care for my mom, and paid Roy and I little attention. But on this occasion, she decided to make an appearance along with my dad's sister, Aunt Joann and her husband, Ralph. My cousins, fraternal twin brothers, Keith and Kenny, played a game of hide and seek with Roy and me outside.

As the smell of charcoal wafted across the yard, we were absorbed in the game, stumbling, and giggling as we found one another and took off running. On our third round, I made my way into the perfect hiding spot in some brush beneath a tree with Scottie by my side. Waiting to be found, I put my arm around Scottie and stared up at the swaying branches and the darkening sky beyond. Then I heard it—a long, shrill scream.

Slowly, we all came out of our hiding spots and huddled together. Keith and Kenny, also raised in a tumultuous home, knew exactly what we were thinking.

*Something bad is happening.*

Scottie in tow, we began to walk toward the house when Big Momma slammed through the door and stomped to her car, peeling out of the driveway, sending plumes of dust into the air as she sped away.

As we got closer to the house, we began to hear pieces of what was going on. Dad was cussing and tearing the house up,

*Slap.*

"Why the fuck did ya say that to her?"

*Thud.*

Knowing that Mom was getting a beating, Roy ran inside to try to get Dad to stop. As soon as Dad caught sight of Roy, he ripped his belt off and began swinging it at him. Roy bolted out of the house. Dad right on his heels, whipping the belt buckle over and over as Roy ran.

"You lard ass, get back here!"

I screamed as the buckle hit Roy all over his body—his back, arms, backside, and eventually his legs. Roy would be left with a knot on his hamstring the size of a large grapefruit. It would later turn into a benign tumor that had to be surgically removed. This was the brute force with which Dad struck. Once he was triggered, he lashed out with all his might, causing mass destruction in the form of cuts, bruises, big fleshy knots, broken glass, and holes in walls. This explosion left my mom and brother bloody and bruised from head to toe. I tried to tend to them, but there was nothing I could do. I brought Scottie inside and started cleaning up the mess as Dad's truck engine roared and he tore out of the driveway. As I picked up broken glass, placed lamps back on tables, and searched for the broom, I finally said goodbye to any shred of hope that our family would ever be a *family*.

Of course, what happened the next day followed a script that we all knew too well. Dad didn't come home. Rumors got back to Mom that my dad had gotten drunk at a bar and gone home with another woman.

Mom succumbed to the darkness.

As the day slid by, I called out for her and couldn't find her. There was an eerie silence as I checked all over the house until, finally, I came to the bathroom door.

"Mom?" I called nervously, trying to push the door open. Something was blocking it. I pushed harder until I noticed what was blocking the door: Mom. I gave the door a shove and it flew open. My breath caught as I saw Mom on the floor sobbing softly with her wrists cut. Blood was trickling down her arms and plopping in big drops on the floor, the stainless-steel razor blade lying next to her. I ran to the phone and called Aunt Ginny who came over to the house immediately. While waiting on my aunt, I silently wrapped mom's wrist with some rags and cleaned the mess.

"It's going to be alright Mommy", I said, trying to soothe her pain.

*"When I grow up, I'll take care of you,"* I muttered.

She sat slumped over, coming in and out of consciousness. When my aunt arrived, she was able to get Mom up and into the car so she could take her to the hospital. Aunt Ginny turned to us, and said, "Go inside and wait for your uncle." Roy and I watched as the car pulled away. My heart was heavy and ached to breathe, I felt drained and empty. Roy was in severe pain from the beating the day before and had been in bed all day. I made my way up to his bedroom, crawled into bed with him, and let the sun warm our faces as we each quietly tried to process what had happened.

Once she reached the hospital and was treated for her injuries, Mom was placed into protective custody for attempting suicide. The court ordered that she be admitted to the state mental hospital in Arcadia, where she received treatment that finally proved helpful. That all started with a proper diagnosis—she was formally diagnosed with manic depression, also known as bipolar affective disorder. As a course of action, they began electroconvulsive therapy, and prescribed her Lithium and Valium.

While Mom was gone, Granny came from Ft. Pierce to stay with Roy and me. She lovingly cared for Roy's injuries. With Granny, away from all the crazy that came with Mom and Dad, we found ourselves blossoming as kids once again, benefitting from the consistent love, constant care, and steady routine Granny provided. However, all the good Granny did for us couldn't erase the fact that we were carrying unprocessed trauma and unwanted labels, both within the family and the community. Aunts, uncles, and cousins whispered about Crazy Janice, while those who barely knew us had already labeled us *white trash*—something I never understood until I overheard it.

Several weeks before Mom went away, I sat in the cafeteria with my free lunch tray in front of me. As I reached to open my orange juice, I overheard an administrator talking to my teacher. "Are Jana Lee's parents coming to the PTA meeting tonight?" she asked.

My teacher responded with a chuckle, "No, they're not coming. They're such white trash."

My face grew red; my cheeks burned. I had no idea what the phrase meant, but I knew it couldn't be good.

That night, while sitting at the kitchen table doing homework with Scottie at my feet, I looked over at Mom and asked, "What's *white trash?*"

She looked up from the pot she was stirring, furrowed her brow and responded, "Where did you hear that?"

"At school. . .my teacher said our family was *white trash*. What does that mean?" I asked.

"It means I'm going to the school tomorrow to show that teacher what white trash really is."

True to her word, Mom marched into the school the next day and cursed my teacher out—thus solidifying what everyone seemed to think about us already. And now, with Mom hospitalized and Dad running around town with a different woman every night, rumors ran rampant. At school I felt different and constantly compared myself to my classmates. My legs wanted to run, my hair wanted to flow in the breeze, my heart beat fast as I pumped my legs on a swing. Yet, as I played, something held me back. My mind constantly churned as I dreamed of finding ways to be like everyone else. Variations of the false beliefs; *I'm not good enough and I'm unwanted,* had become my psyche's operating system.

One night, I sat in my room and stared into the mirror. I looked at my dark brown eyes, my baby fine chin-length blond hair, and smiled revealing several missing and a few half-grown teeth. I stared at my reflection, taking in my secondhand clothes, noticing every small stain on my worn shirt. I looked at Scottie. "Am I ugly?"

He lifted his head, panting softly.

"Scottie, I don't want to be me anymore. I want to be someone else."

He crawled closer to me on his belly, as if he knew I needed to be comforted.

I sniffed. My body ached to feel anything other than the sting of being me. I didn't want to be different. I wanted to be like the beautiful, carefree girls at school with their new clothes and glossed lips. I wanted to experience what it was like to live in a big household filled with love where the parents didn't tear one another apart and where money wasn't scarce. I just wanted to *be.* But there was no way that would ever happen.

Not only was I carrying the labels given to me by others, I was also carrying an entirely new burden: Mom. Seeing her on the floor, her wrists shredded and bleeding, it struck me that she wasn't just stuck in a cycle of drama and heartache with my dad.

*She was fragile.*

*She was weak.*

*She was a victim.*

Those facts alone helped me understand that my life was no longer about living. It was about surviving. It was about growing up fast. It was about being strong so I could take care of Mom.

I sat up and looked down at Scottie whose head was now resting on my knee. "You know, I'm going to take care of Mom, right?"

Scottie glanced up at me.

"When I grow up, I'll take care of her."

Scottie panted.

I closed my eyes and put my arms around him.

"You're my best friend," I whispered.

When Mom finally came home, I could tell that treatment had changed her. Doctors explained to Granny that Mom's brain had been rewired by the electroconvulsive therapy she received. She now seemed capable of so much more. Her energy was stable, and she was expanding herself spiritually. She was no longer only devoted to the church; she was open to new far-reaching ideas that she seemed to eat up. She became fascinated with mystical teachings, and transpersonal psychology. She would sit with Scottie and me and share what she was learning. Dr. Raymond Moody's book *Life After Life* on near death experiences was one of her favorites. Soon she began teaching me to meditate using a 33 black vinyl record of guided meditations she'd been given by a therapist during her hospital stay. She was reading any book she could get her hands on by the "sleeping prophet", Edgar Cayce. She devoured Linda Goodman's *Sun Signs* about astrology. Today, I look back on this time as my mom planting seeds within me that one day, when I was older, took root and grew, blossoming into the teacher I would become.

Though Mom was trying to connect with Roy and me by teaching us new things, she remained emotionally distant and slept a lot—an effect of the high dose of Valium she was prescribed. I often came into her room when she was sleeping, tucked her in, and got a glass of water to put on her bedside table. Sometimes I'd kiss her head. Sometimes I'd run my hands over her thick, dark hair.

*I would whisper to her: "When I grow up, I'll take care of you Mommy."*

For Mother's Day that year I made her a card at school. It read:

*Roses are red.*

*Violets are blue.*

*My Mommy sleeps a lot.*

*And I love her too!*

Mom didn't work after she returned from the hospital; she was taking a disability check from the state. We received food stamps and would shop with them, buying as much as we could for what little we had available. As much as I wanted to care for Mom by helping, I hated going to the store with her. Those food stamps were tangible proof that we were different, that I was trash. I found myself constantly ducking around shelves to avoid being seen. No matter which way I turned, there seemed to be affirmation that I was different, less than, and simply not good enough, further solidifying my false beliefs.

> Depress literally means to "press down or lower." When we aren't connected to our emotions, our 'inner child' and don't have the emotional intelligence to manage the beliefs that create the feelings, we become depressed. Our inner child is our feeling self. When we were under the age of seven, we experienced the world through our emotions. Our brains don't fully develop until our mid-twenties. Small children don't have the rational structures and defenses of an adult. When an emotionally charged event occurred in childhood, we felt alone, helpless and in despair. Children don't know how to process and digest the feelings or experiences, so they make it mean something about themselves or the world. This is how a false belief is formed. What false belief did you adopt from an emotionally charged event in your conditioning years? Examples: "I'm not good enough, I'm unlovable, I don't matter, I'm invisible"

*Chapter 13*

# THE KING

~ *1974* ~

I was playing with my dolls when the phone rang a week after Mom came home from the hospital. I ran to the kitchen to grab the receiver from its place on the wall. "Hello?"

"Can I speak with Janice? This is Mr. Connor, the landlord."

"Mom! It's for you!" I called out.

Mom shuffled into the kitchen in her robe and took the receiver from me. "Hello?"

I stood there and watched as Mom held the phone to her ear, listening intently to Mr. Connor as he spoke. Her breath became quick, her eyes filled with tears. "Okay, I understand," she sighed. "All right, we will. Thank you."

She hung up the phone and sank to the floor.

"Mom, what happened?" I asked, sitting next to her.

"He's selling the place," she said, her voice tight. "We have to move."

Scottie jumped into my lap as I closed my eyes, letting a stream of tears pour down my face. I'd have to say goodbye to the idyllic childhood home—the one thing that made me feel stable and *good*.

The grief took hold and wouldn't seem to lift. Roy and I packed with the feeling of uncertainty as we tried to grasp what was to come. We were saying goodbye to the big grassy fields, our towering trees, and the fish troughs we'd come to love. I was mourning. I felt abandoned by God. Frankly, I was angry at God, why would He allow this to happen? "How much more suffering must I endure?" I pleaded.

The place Mom was able to secure for us for her $300 per month disability check would be nothing like the fish farm, nor was it like anything we'd ever experienced. We'd be moving into a trailer on the outskirts of town, in a 'mobile home' park. I dreaded moving, not only because I loved our two-story home so much, but also because moving into a trailer further affirmed the awful things I felt about myself and my family.

Knowing we were struggling, one day before we moved, Jerry Graves, a childhood friend of my parents who went by the nickname of Buddy (not to be confused with Uncle Buddy), stopped by the house. Buddy Graves was a robust man with a belly that hung over his waistband. He owned a pool hall in town and had a mangled nose, a reminder of the bar fights he'd won and lost. Buddy was secretly in love with Mom and showed it whenever he had the opportunity. Mom had no romantic feelings for him, she viewed him like a brother—someone to care for her when my dad wasn't around. He walked through the door, widened his stance, and waved Mom over to him.

"Janice," he said, his eyes twinkling, "Elvis is coming to town. He's playing tonight at the Lakeland Civic Center!"

"You're kidding me," she responded.

"I got you two tickets! You and Jana Lee can go!"

Overhearing their conversation, my heart began to race. Elvis wasn't just some performer on TV. He wasn't just someone we listened to on the radio—he was a part of us; he was *family*. He was Southern and had grown up poor like us. He was a demi-god in our home and in the homes of our friends and relatives. But, for me, the love I felt ran extra deep; it coursed through my veins. Through his songs, I was able to feel things far too big for my little body. I'd play "Suspicious Minds" over and over on the record player, closing my eyes and imagining my dad as Elvis and my mom as Priscilla. Tears would slide down my face as I tucked my knees into my body and sang the lyrics on the floor of my bedroom. I knew the depths of my parents' love, felt the pain of their breakup, and grieved to the buttery soft sounds of Elvis' voice. He was the force that gave me an early taste of adult emotions.

That night, I played Elvis songs over and over as Scottie sat on my bed and watched me choose the perfect outfit. I decided on a matching set—yellow polyester pants and shirt. Butterflies beat at the walls of my belly as I watched Mom put the finishing touches on her catlike eyeliner, then nearly empty an entire can of hairspray onto her perfectly teased hair. I couldn't stop staring at her reflection through the cloud of hairspray as she straightened her dress and gave herself one last look. She was absolutely stunning—a dead ringer for Priscilla.

*And we were going to see our KING!*

We soon hopped in the car and popped an Elvis 8-track into the car stereo. As we left the fish farm and made our way to the highway, we sang along to every song, dramatically acting out the lyrics at times. By the time we pulled into the Civic Center, we were high on Elvis.

We entered the venue in a crowd of thousands of people, all chatting excitedly. Our seats were behind the stage and up a few rows, giving us a perfect view of Elvis' backside for much of the night. When he came out on stage, the crowd erupted into screams so loud, my ears could hardly handle the volume. But I didn't care—there he was, in the flesh. I was starstruck.

I spent the entire concert oscillating between being there, enjoying every delicious second, and letting each song transport me to a time when our family was happy together. I sang along to "You Don't Have to Say You Love Me", "Can't Help Falling in Love With You", and "Always On My Mind" with tears flowing from my eyes. Woven together, the songs formed the backdrop of my childhood.

*Mom and Dad dancing in the living room.*
*Me cuddled on Dad's lap as he softly sang.*
*Dad's crooked smile.*
*Mom's best Priscilla.*
*Dad's laugh as he shook his hips.*
*"I love you, Time."*

My cheeks soon felt chapped from the tears, my mouth sore from smiling. I couldn't move—I was riveted. I needed to go to the bathroom but forced myself to stay seated so I wouldn't miss anything. It soon became too much, and I released my bladder, then sat for the remainder of the concert in a puddle of warm pee.

Then, as quickly as it began, the concert was over.

*"Elvis has left the building."* The announcer said over the speakers.

Mom took my hand, and we left our seats—mine with a pool of pee beneath it—and headed to our car. Other concertgoers talked about the show and how amazing it was, a few of them mentioning how fat Elvis had gotten. My face reddened and my fists clenched as I heard these comments. *How dare anyone talk about him that way!*

Once we reached the car, still high from our experience, Mom and I hopped inside and began to play the 8-tracks once more. Mom turned the key, and we made our way out of the parking lot and back onto the I-4 headed west. Soon, we were passed by a limousine. Then another.

"Jana Lee, its Elvis, there aren't limousines driving in Central Florida. That's him. That's Elvis!"

"No way," I cried.

"Hold on tight!"

Mom stepped on the gas. Our little 1964 Dodge Dart only went about 60 mph full out. Mom pursued the motorcade, following it all the way to downtown Tampa.

Within the hour, we arrived at the Hilton, just one car length behind the second limo. They pulled around the barricade and stopped. The back window lowered, it was Sweet Inspiration, Elvis' backup singers, which included Whitney Houston's mom, Sissy Houston. They were leaning out the window, waving their arms, motioning for us to leave. Then, something miraculous happened. Someone came up to the security guard and pointed at our car; the guard nodded and walked over and lifted the barricade.

We were directed to the back of the hotel where Elvis was being ushered to his suite. As we drove up, Mom cut the car engine and got out. I watched as Elvis walked slowly over to the security guard. I turned to see his girlfriend, Linda Thompson, the former beauty queen, dressed in a long, backless blue sequin gown walk through the delivery entrance to the hotel.

Mom opened my door and said, "Jana Lee, do you want to get out, sweetheart?"

I let out a sob. "No mommy, please! I have wet stinky pants from peeing. Please no. I can't meet him like this. Don't make me go!"

I could hear Elvis telling the guard to let us know we were invited up to his suite. My throat was tight as Elvis watched the guard approach our car. "Y'all are invited up. Mr. Presley wants to meet you, little girl."

Mom's eyes widened. "Honey, you hear him? Elvis wants to meet you! I bet you remind him of his daughter, Lisa Marie!"

I wiggled in my seat. The urine was still damp on my pants, which were now stained in the crotch. "No, no, Mom. Please."

Elvis beckoned the security guard back over. He unwrapped his blue, silk scarf from his neck, handed it to the guard, and pointed at me. The guard walked back over to the car, handed the scarf to me, and said, "He wants you to have this. He also said to let him know if you change your mind, I can bring you up."

I watched through wet eyes as Elvis walked away. It hurt so deeply, it felt like every time I watched my Daddy walk away. He always walked away.

As we drove toward home, the streetlights sending light bursting through the car, I said quietly, "I'm sorry Mommy, we can do it again when he comes back next year."

Mom chuckled and said, "No, Honey. That was a once in a lifetime chance."

I stared out the window and sighed, burying my face in the smooth silk scarf, letting the smell of Elvis fill me up.

When we were little, we believed anything was possible. We believed we could be an astronaut, an actor, even the president. Yet, we grow up and our conditioning from childhood taints our ability to remember that there are infinite possibilities. What did you believe was possible when you were small, that you now have accepted as impossible?

*Chapter 14*

# LITTLE VIETNAM
## 1974

*"Life is amazing. And then it's awful. And then it's amazing*
*again. And in between the amazing and awful it's ordinary and*
*mundane and routine. Breathe in the amazing, hold on through the*
*awful, and relax and exhale during the ordinary. That's just living*
*heartbreaking, soul-healing, amazing, awful, ordinary life.*
*And it's breathtakingly beautiful."*[7]

—L.R. Knost

I sat backwards staring out the dingy window, watching the fish farm disappear. Scottie chased the car as far as he could, eventually stopping in the brown cloud of dust we left at the end of the driveway. I was devastated, crying out when Mom told us we couldn't bring him to our new home. I sobbed as I imagined him alone outside, pacing the yard, looking for me. I pictured him sitting at the door, crying to get inside, wishing someone would open it for him. I knew that feeling of *wishing*

---

7 L. R. Knost, The Gentle Parent: Positive, Practical, Effective Discipline (Little Hearts
  Books, 2013)

so intimately. I never wanted my best friend in the world to experience that pain.

The car ride was silent. My mind wandered to our new place and what it would be like, all I felt was fear. I closed my eyes and found myself in worship, praying to Jesus to protect us as we moved into our new home. My body swayed with the car's movements as we rounded bends and shifted lanes. I let myself feel comforted by the presence of Spirit.

Finally, we made our way down a dirt path into a neighborhood filled with trailers, each with their own dirt yards. We drove past old, rusting cars, piles of trash on the side of the road, and visibly dirty children playing in their underwear. I felt sick as we pulled up to the trailer, dented and dirty on all sides. The fence was falling apart, patches of grass filled with mounds of sandspurs covered the area surrounding the rusty trailer. As Mom turned the ignition off, I opened my door and got out—the sound of cicadas was almost deafening. Their guttural, undulating groans nearly moved me to tears.

Mom went to the mailbox to retrieve the keys and we slowly walked together toward the door. Once she managed to get the key into the lock, she rattled it until the door popped open. Before we could even step inside, palmetto bugs swarmed us, their thick, unwieldy bodies getting stuck in our hair and clothes. Mom slammed the door and went to the car for a can of Raid. She bounded up the stairs and we followed as she opened the door again. Roy and I stood outside as Mom filled the inside with a thick cloud of poison, sending the palmetto bugs plunging to their deaths.

I tried to steel myself against the emotions that were swelling inside me. I prayed to Jesus, asking Him to take the pain away, but a hot tear slid down my face as shame blanketed my entire body.

*Jana Lee's Family? They're such white trash.*

I kicked the dirt. I balled my fists. I hated this place. At least at the fish farm, I could run fast and far, climbing high into towering trees or getting myself lost in imaginary games. Now, without the magic of the fish farm and the comfort it offered, I was left alone with my shame—shame that continued to increase. My surroundings now matched every hateful thing anyone had ever said about me. I leaned my body against the trailer and squeezed my eyes shut.

Then, there it was: a *whisper*. A small voice inside that quietly urged me to remember that I wasn't *trash, I am a child of God*. I had experienced so much trauma; although I was only eight, my faith was growing, and I was learning that I could face whatever was to come. My heart seemed to expand, swelling with love, my body flooded with warm sensations. I knew this whisper was coming from Spirit. The Creator. In this moment, I was able to put the fear, anxiety, and shame aside and remember that I was loved. And if that was true, then I was worthy of so much more. I also had this newfound awareness, that life is awful and then it's not, that everything is impermanent. Mom would always say, "Jana Lee the only constant in life is change." My favorite Mom saying was, "today is the beginning of the rest of your life." Mom's one-liners would remind me of the truth.

As I sat in the grass, I thought:

*This too shall pass.*

It wasn't long before Mom opened the door and called us inside. Her eyes were bright red. I couldn't tell whether they were red from the Raid, or she had been crying. I suspected it was a combination of the two. Dead and dying palmetto bugs crunched beneath our feet as we walked into the trailer. Though the lights were on, the kitchen was dark—the walls, cabinets, and floors lined with dark wood paneling. There were two small bedrooms one on each end of the trailer. Mom took one, I was given the other, Roy would sleep on the couch in the dingy living room. Together, we took trips to and from the car, slowly moving our things into the filthy trailer. I took my Barbies into my bedroom and dumped them on the floor. With a sinking heart, I whispered, "Welcome home."

That night, Buddy Graves and some of his friends came to help move our bigger furniture inside. With everything inside, the trailer was even more cramped and, somehow, even sadder. It felt like a representation of the state we found ourselves in after years of ups and downs. Mom gave the home a nickname. She called it *Little Vietnam*.

In the weeks that followed, Buddy Graves visited the trailer often to check in. He watched as Roy, Mom, and I tried to navigate this new life without buckling under our grief.

"Okay, everyone, let's get ready!" he shouted, bursting through our door one Saturday morning. "We're going to Walt Disney World!"

Roy and I screamed with delight as Mom gathered her purse and tried to muster a smile.

All the way to Lake Buena Vista, Buddy talked about how much fun we were going to have, the rides, and all the Disney characters we'd meet. When we arrived, Mom took my hand as we made our way through the gates of Magic Kingdom. That's when the magic took hold.

We walked from street to street, each lined with perfect houses. Every house was perfectly painted with big, shiny windows and a wide door with a knocker on it. Each was fitted with a brightly colored window box, lush flowers spilling over.

*I will live in a house like this one day.*

Cinderella, Snow White and Prince Charming wandered around the park, stopping to take photos with excited children. Our favorite characters, Mickey, Donald Duck and Goofy skipped through the streets as happy children crowded them, asking for autographs. Roy and I raced from character to character, ride to ride, filled with big, bubbly happiness that felt like a sugar high. My imagination ran wild as I pictured myself living at the park, waking to the sounds of chirping birds, playing all day, and tucking in at night to the popping of fireworks.

As the sun set, Buddy grabbed our hands and took us to one last magical place: a store that sold Mickey Mouse hats. He bought me one and had my name embroidered on the front. I loved that hat. It reminded me of our special day at Disney World.

Roy shook me awake when we pulled into the trailer park that evening. As we gathered our things from the car, we noticed an animal sitting in our doorway. It was dirty, oddly shaped. We weren't sure what it was. I looked at Roy who shrugged his shoulders and started walking with me toward the door. The animal stood as we approached. We stopped.

*Is that?*

"Scottie!" I called out, running toward him. His coat was matted, his feet cracked and bleeding. He shied away, but with some coaxing, he made his way into my arms. He had traveled more than seven miles to find me. I cried tears of joy—this was proof that my prayers were being heard.

As we settled into the trailer, Roy and I tried to find ways to recapture joy in our day-to-day lives. I was still young enough to find comfort in my imagination, living in dreams of a big, happy family with a picture-perfect Disney home, filled with things we loved. Roy had made neighborhood friends and would spend as much time with them as he could, often leaving the house for hours, sometimes days on end, leaving me all alone. Mom seemed to be returning to us, often waking up and making us our favorite breakfast; grits, sunny-side up eggs and sliced 'maters' in the morning. Her spark had returned. She did the best she could to make the shabby trailer a home. The twinkle in her eye was back. I dreaded what that might mean.

*Of course, I knew.*

Mom, Roy, and I sat down for dinner, while outside, there was a fierce thunderstorm brewing. Since moving into the trailer, my anxiety during storms was becoming debilitating. Mom would do her best to calm me, saying, "Honey that's just God moving furniture." It never worked. Every crashing thunderbolt shook the flimsy trailer. The little protection the metal walls provided seemed inadequate. I didn't feel safe, I imagined the trailer getting struck by lightning, killing all of us, or that a tornado would rip the trailer to pieces.

I jumped at the sound of a knock on the front door. Mom raised her eyebrows. "I wonder who that could be?"

I ran to the door and flung it open. Dad stood on the lowest step, holding a lead. At the other end of the lead was a beautiful, brown horse. "Is he for us?!" I shouted.

Roy came running.

"Yep. This big gah is all yours," Dad responded, his lips curled into his signature crooked smile with a toothpick dangling from the corner of his mouth.

"Thank you, thank you, thank you!" I squealed, hugging Dad around his legs.

"Now both of you git out here 'n' take him into the yard—his name's Billy."

Dad handed me the lead as he walked past Roy and took Mom into his arms, closing the door behind him. With Billy there, I didn't give myself a chance to think about what it meant that Dad had shown up. I was focused on holding the lead, which felt big in my hands.

"C'mon, Billy. Easy now!" I said as I walked slowly into the fenced yard, Billy trailing obediently behind me. Roy followed Billy and me, his eyes cast downward.

I understood why.

This time, there was no honeymoon period. There was no singing and dancing, no stolen kisses, no sweet, loving moments between my mom and dad. It was as if they'd picked up right where they left off. The fighting was nearly constant—Dad's drinking never seemed to stop. He was ratcheting up the verbal abuse towards Roy and beating Mom a few times a week. Roy was only ten years old and began to practically live with neighbors, rarely coming home. Mom fell into deep depression once again. I stayed in my bedroom hiding under the bed when the violence erupted.

Billy quickly became best friends with Scottie and me. I would spend hours brushing and braiding his mane and then cleaning the makeshift barn that sat across the small dirt road, directly in front of our trailer. My friendship with Billy brought me so much joy and calmed my nervous energy which today would have been diagnosed as ADHD. At only eight years old, I was helpless; I couldn't protect him from the reality of what it meant to be a part of our family. On nights when Dad was drunk and angry, he'd beat Billy with his lead so badly that he'd break the skin. Billy eventually tried to escape and got caught up in the barbed wire fencing Dad had installed around the barn area. The lacerations looked angry and infected for weeks afterward. Every evening, Roy and I would go outside to the barn and dab petroleum jelly on his wounds. He would nudge us and 'blow' releasing the pent-up stress. I would whisper "I love you", doing my best to soothe his pain.

One evening, as I stood brushing his mane, I said, "I miss the fish farm. You would have loved it there. There was so much space, so much room to play. The big trees were my favorite. I loved to climb—"

I stopped brushing and placed my hand on Billy's chest as I heard it. Rising voices coming from inside the trailer.

"It's okay, Billy. I'll go see what's happening."

I pulled myself up and peeked into the window. There was Dad, standing over Mom who sat on the couch, nodding obediently. Roy stood behind the kitchen table, frozen, staring at Mom and Dad. I wasn't sure whether I should run and hide or go inside and stand next to Roy, but something called me to go in. I walked up the stairs and pushed the door open. Right as I opened the door, I heard it.

*Slap.*

I ran to Roy's side and grabbed his arm hiding behind him.

Dad yanked a book from Mom's stack on the side table and threw it at her face. "Ya think this shit makes you smart, whore?"

"No," Mom whispered.

"Ya know what? Git up. Git the fuck up." He reached out and wrenched

91

Mom off the couch by her collar.

Dad dragged Mom outside and shoved her down on the ground. Roy and I followed, shouting, "No!" and "Stop Dad!" over one another.

Mom sat huddled on the side of the small dirt road as Dad stooped down and shouted in her face, "You're a cock-suckin' cunt, you know that?"

I looked around. The street was desolate, the only light coming from the windows of other trailers.

"I'm gonna teach you a lesson!" Dad reached down and grabbed Mom by the hair this time and flung her onto the road. She landed splayed out, her body scraping against the dirt and gravel. Then he stomped toward his pickup, swaying as he went.

Roy and I ran to Mom's side, trying to get her up, yet she was limp and heavy, weeping. "Momma, get up now!" Roy shouted, shaking her.

"Daddy, STOP!" I screamed. "STOP!"

Dad jumped into his truck and revved the engine, backing out of his spot in front of the trailer. His headlights blinded us as he threw his truck into gear then hurdled toward us. Panicked, Roy and I jumped out of the way as he hit the gas.

"NO! NO!" Roy and I screamed in unison.

Barely six inches before his tires hit Mom, he slammed on the brakes. Roy and I ran to her side as Dad opened his door and tumbled out of the driver's seat. "Ya got it, bitch?"

Mom lay lifeless.

"I SAID, DO YOU GOT IT, BITCH?"

Mom nodded her head.

"Good. Cause next time, I'll finish the job."

Later that night as Roy and I comforted Mom, Dad crashed through the front door. He shoved his way into my room and grabbed my Mickey Mouse hat off my bed. He grabbed his bottle of whiskey, stumbled outside, and walked toward the barn. Tending to Mom, I barely noticed Dad yanking Billy out of the stable. He placed my hat on Billy's head, tucking the elastic under his chin. He then mounted Billy and trotted off, swigging the whiskey as he rode. We heard later from Buddy Graves, that when he arrived in town, police officers surrounded him, and eventually got him off the horse and into a squad car. Dad was arrested for public intoxication and animal cruelty.

This time, there was no real breakup. Dad was just gone. We never saw Billy again.

# Chapter 15

# BARREL

## 1974

Dad had always been a womanizer, but once he got out of jail, he started dating someone more quickly (and more publicly) than usual. Her name was Janey, and she was a known prostitute. The mental wellness and relative emotional stability my mom experienced following her stay at the institution, now felt like a distant memory. She was so spun out about Dad's relationship with Janey that she could barely catch any rest. Mom slipped further and further into depression and soon found herself in the deepest, darkest cavern of her life. I hadn't experienced this version of Mom. It was as if all the accumulated mental, emotional, and physical abuse combined with yet another rejection by Dad, pushed her over a cliff. She slept all day; she didn't cook for us or wake us up for school. Roy and I had to fend for ourselves. Dinner consisted of Roy cooking some Spaghetti-O's, hotdogs or TV dinners. When night fell, Mom would shake Roy and I awake, hustling us into the Dodge Dart, driving around to local bars looking for Dad. On the nights when she couldn't find him, she'd come home and cry for hours, curled into a ball on the couch in the lamplight. The nights when Mom did manage to find Dad, things were even worse.

One night, I awoke next to Roy in the backseat. I nudged him awake as I heard screaming and shouting. We looked through the windshield to see Dad shoving Mom out of the bar's swinging door. He pushed her up against the wall choking her and yelling in her face, "Who the hell d'you think ya are, followin' me like this?"

He slapped her across the face and pushed her harder against the wall. "You bitch!"

*Slap.*

"Fuck you!"

*Slap.*

"You whore!"

Roy and I held one another and prayed as a stranger pulled Dad off Mom.

"Jesus, please save us," I prayed as I wrung my hands in terror. The police arrived, but nothing was done. Back then domestic violence was viewed as a nuisance, not an actual crime.

It was a sweltering Saturday afternoon when Dad pulled up too Little Vietnam in his girlfriend's new Lincoln Continental. He stepped out of the car and lit a cigarette, took a deep drag, and called for Roy and me.

"Please, Mom, don't make me go," Roy pleaded. "Please?"

"You have to go," Mom replied, emotionless.

I understood Roy's hesitation—I also had a sick feeling about going, but I was able to push that aside. Dad had promised to take us to a restaurant to eat, which was my favorite thing to do. I also couldn't wait to ride in his new car, which was bright and shiny, reflecting the sunlight.

"It's okay, Roy," I said, resting my hand on his arm. "We're going together."

We opened the door and walked outside, the heat hitting our faces like a hot, wet washcloth.

"Hey, Time," Dad called out, flicking his cigarette to the ground.

I slowly walked over to him.

He picked me up and hugged me, then put me on the ground. I flung the door open and slid in next to Roy who was already inside. The car smelled brand new and felt safe and cool. I reached over and nudged Roy who stared out the window.

We pulled out of the driveway and headed toward town. My mouth watered as I imagined biting into a hot, salty cheeseburger, and pictured washing it down with a root beer float. Yet, as we drove, one by one, every restaurant in town flashed by the window.

"Dad, aren't we gonna to stop to eat?"

"Nah, not today," he responded.

Instead, we drove to Janey's trailer in Lakeland. Dad ushered us out of the car and guided us to the door. When we walked in, our eyes fell on posters of naked men covering the walls in the living room. We then peeked down to the end of the trailer where more posters of naked women hung. I felt lightheaded. I grabbed onto Roy's arm.

"Daddy, I feel scared. Can we go home?" I asked, my face flushed.

"Hell no!" he hollered. "We just got here, Jana Lee."

Janey walked into the room and kissed Dad passionately. She had dark skin, and black hair teased high, gold jewelry adorned her neck and wrists. Roy and I muttered, "Hi" in unison, looking down at the floor. As soon as my dad turned his attention back to her, we disappeared outside and sat with our backs against the trailer in the heat, hungry and sad. My mind raced. I had never seen a naked man. I kept trying to make sense of why an adult would have pictures of naked people all over the walls—it seemed so gross. I looked over at Roy. He sat with a grimace on his face, quietly tearing weeds out of the sandy ground.

Hours went by before Dad stepped out of the trailer and said, "Git in the car. Time to get you shits back to yo' Mammy."

Without a word, we drove back to Little Vietnam. The car no longer felt safe or smelled wonderful—its scent repulsed me. When we pulled up to the trailer, Dad didn't say goodbye or even wave to us. He waited for us to get out of the car then tore out of the driveway as if he was leaving trash by the side of the road. Before Roy and I walked inside, we'd agreed to say nothing about what happened with Dad. We knew it would cause more fighting and we wanted to avoid that at all costs.

As we opened the door, we heard music—Johnny Cash, singing "A Thing Called Love" —on the radio. We also heard voices chatting; Mom had a friend over. Roy and I headed right to the kitchen and dug through the fridge to gather supplies for tomato and mayonnaise sandwiches.

I placed two slices of bread on a plate just as Mom emerged from the bathroom wearing heavy makeup. Her lips were cherry red, her eyelids a shade of emerald green, and her hair teased 5-inches high.

"Where did you two go with Dad?" she abruptly asked with a slur.

"Nowhere," I answered, barely looking up.

"Well, what happened?"

"Nothing happened," Roy responded, already biting into his sandwich.

"Hmm," Mom murmured and headed back into the bathroom. Because Mom took Valium, she didn't drink. The combination could be dangerous, however, tonight she *was* drinking. We heard laughter and the sound of Mom and her friend bumping into the walls.

Once Roy and I finished our sandwiches, we went outside to play. We grabbed sticks and tried to hit one another in the ankles, laughing as we ran. Soon, Mom called through a window, "Roy! Jana Lee! Get in here!" We dropped our sticks and walked inside. Hauntingly calm, Mom led us one by one into the kitchen and had us stand next to one another, shoulder to shoulder. She then turned and picked up a shotgun—the one she kept in her closet for protection.

She annunciated her words sternly, "I am going to ask you again and this will be the last time I ask. What happened with your dad today? Where did he take you? Who was there?"

The blood drained from my body.

My heart began to race, I broke into a sweat.

"Mom—" I started.

She steadied herself.

She raised the gun.

She touched the barrel to my head.

It was cold.

She slowly shifted the barrel until it touched Roy's head.

Then she stepped back.

She kept the barrel trained on our chests, moving back and forth between Roy and me.

Her feet were planted on the floor.

Her finger was on the trigger.

She drew a breath.

"I want to know, right now, what happened while you were with Dad."

"Nothing happened Mom, we just. . ." Panicked, Roy desperately spoke, quickly blurting every detail of what had gone on.

Mom listened, glaring at us.

Roy continued, talking as fast as he could, trying to calm the situation, but it did nothing.

Mom interrupted, "Boy, I know you're lying!" Her eyes were vacant as she spoke. Mom wasn't there, something evil had taken her over.

Unaware of what exactly was taking place, Mom's friend casually called from the bathroom, "Janice, come on! Let's finish getting ready."

Silence.

Mom raised her voice over the music.

"What did you do with him?"

I couldn't hold my bladder any longer—urine ran down my legs and pooled on the linoleum.

She gritted her teeth.

She steadied the gun.

"Please, Mommy please," I cried. "Nothing happened!"

Roy interjected, "Really, nothing, Mom. Nothing happened. We just met the lady Dad was with—Janey. But nothing happened. We just met her, that was all."

Mom's friend came out of the bathroom. Her eyes locked on the gun as she took in what was happening. She walked slowly toward Mom. "Janice, what are you doing? Give me the gun!"

My body was uncontrollably shaking.

Roy was still desperately talking.

Mom's friend stepped forward and grabbed the gun.

Roy and I held onto one another as Mom collapsed to the floor. Her friend ran to the phone and called my Aunt Ginny, who was at our house within minutes. Aunt Ginny told Roy and I to get into the backseat of her car. She guided Mom into the front seat. When my aunt finally started driving, Mom tried to open the door to jump out. Aunt Ginny had her finger pressed on the passenger lock button pleading with her. "Janice! STOP!" she cried out, grabbing onto Mom's arm and wrestling her while somehow keeping the car steady. It was complete chaos.

We stayed at Aunt Ginny's house that night—Roy and I sharing a bed. We barely slept, trying to make out words as we listened to the adults talking to one another in the living room.

*She has to go.*

*She's not okay.*

*. . .dangerous.*

*She's having another nervous breakdown.*

*What about the kids?*

*Foster care?*

Once I'd heard that, I couldn't unhear it. Aunt Ginny didn't want us.

The next day, my mom was admitted once again to the state psychiatric hospital in Arcadia—this would be her second stint there in a year. As we watched the car pull out of Aunt Ginny's driveway, Mom held her hand flat on the window; tears rolling down her face, while she mouthed 'I'm sorry.' Roy had his arm tightly around me as we both cried. We were completely drained. After everything that had gone on—all that we had been through with our parents—we were now alone in the world. At least we had each other.

## Chapter 16

# ALARM

### 1975

It seemed that Roy and I were destined for misery. The very next day, we were separated. Roy went home with my Uncle Buddy. Uncle Buddy was the only stable father figure I had in my life. A commercial fisherman, he was the quintessential man's man. Roy and I would sit nearby as he cleaned fish, teaching us how to hold the tail firmly and run a descaling tool from tail to head, scraping the scales off. He'd say, "Jana Lee, sit still Honey and hold the fish like this." I would squirm and squeal, the slimy fish and stinky smell repulsed me.

Although Uncle Buddy calmly but sternly let Aunt Ginny and her husband Uncle Bob know that we were *absolutely not* going to foster care. I couldn't go home with him. Uncle Buddy wanted to take me, but he and Gloriana were married, and after the fight between her and my mom, I always felt uneasy around her.

It was decided that I would stay with Aunt Ginny and Uncle Bob, and my two cousins. Diana and Darla were fraternal twins who were fourteen at the time. They reminded me of the sinister pair of Siamese cat sisters in Disney's *Lady and the Tramp* movie, relishing in my suffering. I was scared to live under the same roof as them. They were privileged and lived in a world I only visited on rare occasions.

Aunt Ginny was the opposite of my mom. Whereas Mom was fragile after the death of their daddy, Aunt Ginny was older, and less affected by his death. She was the first in their family to attend college; in Rhode Island—*where all the Yankees are*, according to Granny—Aunt Ginny was a proper southern lady. She prided herself on running an efficient home and an extremely successful pulpwood business with her husband, Uncle Bob. He was a wealthy man; he had been her boss and she was his secretary. The rumor in the family was that they had a long affair, which eventually led him to leave his wife and sons for Aunt Ginny. Most days Uncle Bob stayed in his bedroom. Years later, I would learn that he had been addicted to prescription pain pills. My cousins and aunt walked on eggshells around him. The climate of the house was centered around his moods.

On the night of the incident, when we pulled up outside the house, Roy and I were in awe—the same way we always were when we visited Aunt Ginny. The house was so grand that, despite what we had just experienced, we still marveled. Aunt Ginny punched in the code at the gate, which opened slowly to reveal the enormous estate. The massive, ranch-style, light brick home was lit up, warm and welcoming. As the grownups ushered Mom into a bedroom and settled into the living room to talk, Diana and Darla showed Roy and me their bedrooms. Now, just one day later, I was told I'd be staying there. I wanted to feel excited. I longed to snoop around the house, to handle the objects of art collected on their vacations, and ogle at photos of their Cessna airplane (Aunt Ginny had her pilot's license). I wanted to feel thrilled at the chance to call this mansion home. I wanted to *want* to be there. Yet I just wanted to go home, even though I didn't know where home was anymore.

That Monday morning, there was a storm front coming in, big dark clouds gathered in the sky. I stood waiting in the driveway for the driver; my aunt said would take me to school. I was dressed head-to-toe in new clothes she'd bought for me—even my backpack was new, the straps thick and stiff, pressing into my shoulders. Soon, a shiny black Cadillac with dark tinted windows glided through the gate and stopped right in front of me. The driver got out, rushed to my side of the car, and opened the door. Aunt Ginny placed her hands on my back and guided me into the car. I crawled inside, taking in the smell of cologne and leather, and dropped my backpack. I overheard my aunt speaking to the driver as I buckled my seatbelt.

"Go straight to the school and make sure you watch her walk in," she said.

"Yes, ma'am, not a problem."

"Listen, we're nervous enough about her father trying to take her that we won't let her *near* a school bus. You need to be vigilant," she added.

I stared out the window as Aunt Ginny continued to instruct the driver about what to look out for. My guts twisted. Even though I felt nauseous as I thought about it, a little part of me wanted to be rescued.

I imagined Dad, mad as hell, stomping up to the car at a red light, flinging the driver's door open, grabbing the driver, and pulling him close to Dad's face while belting out an Elvis tune, "You looking for trouble? You came to the right place. You looking for trouble? Just look in my face." That image made me smile.

I tried as hard as I could to settle into life at Aunt Ginny's house, and she tried her best to parent me in the absence of my mom and dad. The trouble was, she wasn't fit to parent someone like me. She was preoccupied managing Uncle Bob's addiction and simply wasn't capable of properly handling a traumatized child. I was spending almost all my time at Aunt Ginny's feeling abandoned, lost and alone. Life at home with my mom had always been tumultuous, but it was familiar. I knew the smell of every one of the meals she cooked and the way she looked in the lamplight, her back against the arm of the couch as she read or watched the *Merv Griffin Show*. I knew her nuances. I knew *her*. I had learned to adapt in survival mode to anticipate my mom's moods. Now, in this new place, I was lost in a vast array of the unfamiliar.

It didn't help that I was unable to get my cousins to include me. Diana and Darla knew very little about my life or why I was staying at their house. All they knew was Aunt Jan was sick, she was mentally unstable, and fragile. I wanted so badly to be accepted by them both, yet I never felt good enough. I hated feeling so insecure and alone. They would race around the estate on their golf cart, with their girlfriends laughing, not a care in the world. It reminded me of my life with Roy, who I desperately missed. I knew that if he were with me, we'd find trees to climb, bugs to catch, and other ways to escape. But I was alone, trying my best to become a version of me that they would like. But it never worked with them. As teenagers, they were entirely uninterested in their traumatized little cousin. Being around them was a steady reminder that, despite my surroundings, one thing would never change: I believed *I was unwanted... trash.*

Although I had more material comforts than I could have ever imagined, I never settled. I was always on edge. It was as if Aunt Ginny believed just giving me 'stuff' would heal me. I was picked up in the new shiny Cadillac every day and brought to school where I was enjoying showing off my new clothes. Many nights, food was brought in from the best restaurants in town, my aunt would constantly nag me to get my elbows off the table and sit up *like a lady*. Diana and Darla in unison would sing-song the jump rope rhyme:

"*Mabel, Mabel, strong and able,*
*Keep your elbows off the table,*
*This is not a horse's stable,*
*But a fancy dining table.*"

This would only further solidify my feelings of not being good enough. On weekends when he was unmedicated, Uncle Bob would give me swimming lessons in the pool. In the evenings, I'd take a bath, change into pajamas—or *nightclothes* as Aunt Ginny called them—and crawl into one of the twin beds in the guest room.

One night, a few days after the incident, I stared at the ceiling, searching for imperfections in the bright white paint. The longer I stared, the heavier my eyelids became.

*Licking a dab of jelly off my fingers.*

*Mom.*

*A nudge on my shoulder.*

*Roy's arm grazing mine.*

*Cold steel on my forehead.*

*My heart hammering in my chest.*

*Mom steadying herself.*

*Her eyes.*

*Fixed.*

*Vacant.*

*Bang!*

My eyes opened. I bolted upright. The crisp white sheets I was lying on were now wet, the mattress soaked. I crawled out of bed and wiggled out of my pajamas, then rooted around in the chest of drawers until I found something to slip on. Unsure of what to do, I crawled into the other twin bed in the room, my heart racing. There was no way I could hide this, nor could I explain it away. I squished my eyes shut and turned to my side, then the other side, then back again. Then, suddenly, I noticed a form standing in the doorway. There stood a woman with blonde hair, gazing at me lovingly. I rubbed my eyes in disbelief. Yet there she stood, smiling softly. "Was it an angel?" I was nervous for a moment, then I felt my body relax. The woman came toward me and stood at the edge of the twin bed.

*Am I dreaming?*

"Everything is going to be okay," she said quietly.

"How do you know?" I responded.

"You won't understand now, but one day, when you're older, you will."

I blinked hard to steady myself, lingering for a moment with my eyes closed.

*Am I awake or sleeping?*

When I blinked my eyes open, she was gone.

When the sun came up the next day, I threw the comforter over my stained sheets and still-wet mattress before heading out the door for school. I tried to focus on what my teacher was saying, yet it was difficult. The lack of support for the trauma I had been through left me feeling empty, frazzled and disconnected. It was as if I was witnessing myself from above, disassociated. Every once in a while, I'd think back to the evening before, to my visitor. As much peace as she gave me, I wondered what else I would have to endure before things would feel *okay*.

When I got home, my aunt was waiting in the doorway. "Jana Lee, did you think I wouldn't find out about what you did?"

Darla nudged Diana with her elbow.

"What do you mean?" I gulped.

"Your bed. It was soaked in pee."

"I—" I stammered.

"I don't want to hear it. Your almost nine years old. How can you still be wetting the bed young lady?"

Darla burst out laughing.

"Jana Lee, this better not happen again!"

Mortified, I ran to my room, tears streaking the side of my face. I didn't know what to do, where to go, or who I could turn to. I had nothing. I had no one.

I was experiencing post-traumatic stress disorder and it was manifesting as bed-wetting. I didn't feel safe and desperately needed counseling.

What I thought would be a one-time thing turned into something that persisted. Nearly every night, I was going to sleep and waking up in a puddle of pee. I'd tried everything to make it stop, including limiting how much liquid I drank, but nothing helped. It was as if my body was so tense during the day that it simply let everything go at night.

Finally at the end of her rope, Aunt Ginny told me she was *done with my behavior* and bought a device that would fix the problem once and for all. The machine was a pad with a long wire connected to an alarm. Any time liquid hit the pad, the alarm would go off. That would alert her, Uncle Bob, and my cousins to come into the room to ridicule me for *misbehaving*. Every night, I did everything I could to stay awake to prevent my body from relaxing into sleep. But inevitably, I began to drift.

*Jana Lee, where are you?*

*I stood behind the bathroom door.*

*Jana Lee?*

*Mom walked past the door into the living room.*

*I stifled a giggle.*

*Jana Lee, where did you go?*

*She walked out the front door.*

*I released my breath and started laughing.*

*I came out from behind the door.*

*I sat on the toilet.*

*I smiled wide as I relieved my bladder.*

I nearly fell out of bed as the alarm bell rang, cutting the night's silence like shattering glass. Before I could get my bearings, the door flung open, and Aunt Ginny threw the lights on with Darla in tow. Aunt Ginny was angry. Darla laughed and jeered. I wanted to stand up and scream, "STOP!" I wanted to explain that this wasn't bad behavior, I couldn't help it. I was hurting. I just had a shotgun to my head! This was my body's way of dealing with it. But I was only a child, I didn't know why I couldn't hold my bladder. I was chronically living in a stressed state of fight or flight.

With the machine in use, days crawled by. Things became tense in the household—I felt like the target of a cruel game. Night after night, the bell would sound, footsteps would follow, my eyes filling with tears as my family members pointed and shamed me, my aunt scolding me harshly. Humiliation was all they offered—no encouragement. There was no one in the house who wanted to help me heal. They were all disconnected from me, but really, they were disconnected from themselves and from God. They hadn't been *slain in the Spirit* like I had.

I was their imperfect inconvenience.

It was a warm Saturday, and the family was outside at the pool. Unable to take it anymore, I was spending every moment choking on the lump in my throat. As Uncle Bob and Aunt Ginny swam laps, Diana and Darla lay on the pool deck on top of a foil liner, slathered in baby oil. I walked into the kitchen and tip-toed across the floor to the phone. I picked up the receiver and dialed, then crouched next to the wall. The phone crackled to life, "Hello?"

"Granny?" I whispered.

"Jana Lee! How are you, Sweetheart?" she chirped.

"Granny please come get me. I can't stay here anymore—" I sobbed.

"Why, Honey?" she asked.

"Just come get me. Please?"

"What's going on?"

"I really need you to come now," I said urgently.

I heard rustling on the other end of the line, then the jingling of keys. "I'm getting my things," she said. "Just hang in there, I'll be there soon. I love you."

I hung up the phone then sank down the wall. My body relaxed for the first time since I had been in that house. I closed my eyes and let myself imagine being in Granny's arms, the smell of her, the type of love she gave. After so many weeks of sharp corners and cold hearts, I needed her warmth and softness.

A few hours later, Granny was outside the gate. Surprised, Aunt Ginny buzzed her in. I watched from my bedroom window as Granny pulled into the large, circle driveway, parked in front of the house, and got out.

"Hi, Virginia!" Granny called out, "I got a call from Jana Lee. She, okay?"

Aunt Ginny flung her hands in the air dramatically. "She's fine, what did she say?"

"She said she wants to leave. I'm here to get her," Granny said with a smile.

"Mother, Jana Lee and Roy need to be in foster care. The longer we spend taking care of those kids, the more we enable Janice."

"Virginia, you need to stop it right now. These are *kids*. They're not *things* to use to punish anyone. Let alone your sister."

"Exactly! They're kids. They need to be in a safe place where Janice doesn't have access to them. And don't even get me started on Archie, we've been so scared of him coming by and trying to snatch up Jana Lee—"

"Okay, that's enough. Let me see my girl."

I came out of my room and ran into Granny's arms. She bent down and kissed my head. "Let's get your things Honey." Diana and Darla stood nearby glaring at me as I put my belongings in the car.

Getting into Granny's car was already like being home. She rolled down the windows, lit a Pall Mall and pulled out of the driveway. I watched in the side mirror as Aunt Ginny's grand house disappeared. My little body could hardly handle the relief I felt. My mouth relaxed into a smile. I closed my eyes and let the booming air from the windows caress my face. On the way back to Ft. Pierce, Granny stopped at her favorite restaurant – Jimbo's BBQ in Lakeland. We feasted on barbeque ribs, coleslaw, homemade pickles, and cornbread. My heart was at peace. I was back with my Granny.

Life with Granny on the east coast was starkly different from living with Aunt Ginny. Although I still missed my brother and my mom, I felt peaceful and safe with Granny. I could begin to heal. She enrolled me in the local elementary school which was predominately black. I was now the minority. I quickly made friends with a classmate named Gina. Granny would offer her a ride home after school when she picked me up. Some days, Gina would come with us, but she'd hide in the floorboard of the backseat until we were far from school so no one would see her with the 'white folks'.

In many ways I felt more comfortable with my black friends. I remember when I was four standing in the welfare line waiting for processed cheese and bread to be handed out; Mom would look down at me and say, "Jana Lee, we have more in common with the black folk. Always remember, you ain't better than no one." All I knew was that I rarely felt judged by them. They accepted me. I was never ridiculed for wearing the same outfit to school three times in a week or called white trash. These insults were the norm for me in the predominantly white schools I'd attended in Plant City. In high school, I would spend many weekends at the community center on the 'other side of the tracks', dancing to Prince, Michael Jackson and The Sugar Hill Gang. By then, I had another new label attached to me: *'N'lover*.

At my granny's I'd wake up and rub the sleep from my eyes before skipping down the hallway for a hot, buttery, buttermilk biscuits. She'd spend long days at the barber shop where she worked, so after school I'd go to one of her sisters' houses—Aunt Beatie or Aunt Irma—who cradled me with the same kind of soft, silky love.

Granny and I spent many of her days off in her vegetable garden. She taught me how to dig a hole in the rich soil and lay the seeds, gently covering them. I would run errands with her, picking up fresh, catch of the day from the local fisherman down at the wharf. My favorite dish she'd cook for me, was flounder stuffed with devil crab. On the weekends when Granny wasn't working at the barber shop, she would take me to museums, the beach and miniature golf. Sometimes I would get the extra special treat of dinner at Red Lobster. I'd tie the bib around my neck and slurp lobster meat from the shells, my chin dripping with slick butter. Every night she would read to me and let me sleep with her, my head nuzzled into her soft body. With her nurturing care and unshakeable love, my mind and body healed.

*I never wet the bed again.*

I lived in this peaceful, loving environment for most of my fourth grade. Then, one day as I played in my room, the phone rang, I heard Granny talking to Uncle Buddy about my mom being released from the hospital. I hadn't seen Mom in nearly a year. I was petrified.

Granny sat me down at the table and said, "Jana Lee, your mom is better now Honey and wants you to come home with her and Roy."

I began to cry; I didn't want to go back with her. Granny held me as I sobbed. "Please Granny, NOOOO", I cried.

A few hours later, there was a knock at the front door. I heard Granny open it, then there were murmurs. I instantly recognized the voice.

*She's coming with me.*

*Please, don't take her. Granny begged.*

*She's my daughter*

*You have no choice.*

*She's mine.*

Granny's hands were tied. We cried and held each other as my mom carried my things from the house to the car. Granny urged Mom to stay the night and get on the road the next morning. But Mom wouldn't hear of it. She was quiet and determined in her task at hand.

*Cold steel.*

*What did you do with him?*

*Please, Mommy, NO.*

My whole body was tense. I didn't want to be with her, but I pasted a smile on my face as we got into the car. I was terrified to show Mom that I didn't want to be with her for fear of what she would do to me once Granny wasn't there.

I wanted to jump out of the car and run back, beat on the door, and collapse into her lap, but I sat still, watching her house disappear in the side view mirror. I felt sick.

Goodbye safety and stability.

*Chapter 17*

# STARTING OVER
## ∽ *1976* ∽

*"Not Christian or Jew or Muslim, not Hindu,*
*Buddhist, Sufi, or Zen. Not any religion*
*or cultural system. I am not from the East*
*or the West, not out of the ocean or up*
*from the ground, not natural or ethereal, not*
*composed of elements at all. I do not exist,*
*am not an entity in this world or the next,*
*did not descend from Adam or Eve or any*
*origin story. My place is placeless, a trace*
*of the traceless. Neither body or soul.*
*I belong to the beloved, have seen the two*
*worlds as one and that one call to and know,*
*first, last, outer, inner, only that*
*breath breathing human being."*[8]

—Rumi

---

8  Rumi, The Essential Rumi, ed. Coleman Barks (Harper Collins, 1995)

Upon my return to Plant City with Mom, Granny helped her buy an acre of land with yet another small, shabby trailer on it, in an area outside of town called Turkey Creek. The land was flat with big, old trees lining the largely open property. I stood in the driveway, fighting back hot tears from spilling onto my cheeks.

The air was heavy, weighed down with moisture, mosquitos swirling around and biting my legs. The trees rife with mockingbirds and other songbirds, chattering loudly, speaking a language only they know. My heart yearned for my granny. I braced myself and made my way inside the trailer, which reminded me so much of Little Vietnam that it made my heart drop. Little light filtered through the dirty windows. The dark linoleum floors and cabinets were covered with a layer of greasy filth. I closed my eyes and shook my head. It smelled stale and stagnant, like no one had been there for many years. Mom had been gone for so long, so much had happened, and now, here we were, back in another trailer, starting over *again*.

While Mom was busy bringing things from her car to the trailer, I began to walk along the property line, looking for the perfect tree to climb. I stopped at the base of an enormous oak tree with Spanish moss draping the limbs, I reached for the lowest branch. I struggled to pull myself up, eventually settling on a thin but sturdy branch near the middle of the tree.

I rested my head back and gazed up through the branches into the blue sky with huge, pillowy, white clouds drifting by. I began exploring my imaginary world. I needed to turn inside and disassociate from the pain I was feeling being back here. Later in life when I read an Einstein quote, "Imagination is more important than knowledge. Knowledge is limited. Imagination encircles the world." I understood perfectly how I managed to transform my life in such miraculous ways.

*My imagination was my superpower.*

Just as I was imagining I was back at the beach in Ft. Pierce building a sandcastle, I was startled by the sound of gravel crackling in the driveway. I looked up as Uncle Buddy's pickup pulled up and parked next to the chain-link fence surrounding the trailer.

*Roy!!*

I climbed down the tree, letting myself drop from a branch that was just low enough. Then, I took off running, pulling wisps of moss from my hair as I let my feet fly. When I got to his side, I nearly knocked him to the ground, throwing my arms around him yelling, "ROY!"

"Hi!" he exclaimed.

Uncle Buddy lifted me up into a tight hug, then put me back down and said, "You kids go play, I'm gonna help your mom."

I grabbed Roy by the arm and pulled him along with me. He was getting too old to play with me like he used to, but he picked up a stick and walked the tree line with me, hitting piles of brush and tapping the trees as we went. Roy and I hadn't seen one another in months. Uncle Buddy had brought him to visit Granny and I once in the year I lived with her. We walked in silence, too worn out to imagine what could be next for our frayed, broken family. We never spoke about the night of the gun incident; we couldn't bring ourselves to talk about it—not even a mention.

Mom was stable for a short while after the second hospital stay. The electroconvulsive therapy seemed to work again, allowing her to remain calm and engaged with Roy and me. We got back to quality time watching our favorite television shows, playing card games, and sharing about our day. However, the problem with ECT is that if the environment and the patterns of thoughts and behaviors don't change, the patient will regress. Of course, Mom's circumstances hadn't changed at all. After treatment, she found herself right back in a ramshackle trailer with her two kids just miles away from all the drama that exists in a small town. People still gossiped about Crazy Janice and Archie, who continued to run around town with a different woman each night. Mom couldn't escape it.

Roy and I couldn't help but notice our mom struggling as she worked to find her footing. During the day, she would work in her garden and plant tomatoes, collard greens, and black eye peas. In the evening, she'd put handfuls of collards seasoned with pork fat in the pressure cooker—as they cooked, the trailer filled with the savory, smoky smell of the pork. We would then gather at the table and feast on sweet, buttered cornbread and collards, always with sliced 'maters' on the side. Once we finished dinner, Roy and I would clean the kitchen, or when he was out with friends, I'd clean it myself while Mom watched "The Sonny & Cher Comedy Hour" on the couch until she drifted off to sleep.

It went on like this for months—a steady flow of things that *resembled* normalcy. Each day Mom would walk me to my elementary school nearby. As she left, feelings of abandonment would overcome me. I would begin to hyperventilate and cry, begging her to take me back home.

My teeth were horribly overcrowded; my clothes and shoes were either hand-me-downs from my cousins that didn't fit or Goodwill's 'finest'. I just couldn't compete with other kids my age. Because of this, I couldn't be fully myself around anyone, so I would tell lies about my life and make up stories. Most of the kids knew I was lying and would gather at recess and make fun of me. I'd developed such a vivid imagination that I spent most of my life lost, living in a make-believe world. I'd imagine what my life would be like when I was older. I pictured the house I'd live in, the places I'd visit, the way my journey would unfold. I'd spend days among the trees in nature, dreaming of a life of harmony, blessings and abundance.

It was on a school field trip to a nature center on the Hillsboro River when I felt the most profound connection to the trees and the river. All time stood still, tears rolled down my cheeks. A feeling of bliss washed through me. Nature became my temple; I felt the deepest sense of connection with Spirit when I was in the solitude of the woods

At home, Mom seemed fairly content, but as time marched on, that contentment began to shift. She was still taking a disability check from the State and using food stamps. She had too much time on her hands, as they say, 'An idle mind, is the devil's playground.' Her mood began to shift—highly elevated. We'd walk into the house after school to find her singing to herself while organizing books, magazines, or trinkets on shelves. She'd sway and giggle while cooking. On one trip to a department store, she picked up a sheer, black fringed shawl and put it in her purse. As we walked out the door, I said, "Mommy you didn't pay for that." She shushed me and kept walking. It was obvious she wasn't taking her meds. She was in a manic state. Her mood was consistently. . . good. As the weeks passed, Roy and I began to give one another panicked, pained looks. We knew exactly what this meant.

*Dad.*

Sometimes, Dad's returns were quiet. He'd slide back into family life like he'd never been gone. He'd walk on eggshells for a bit, be on his best behavior, and turn on the charm. I don't have many memories of my dad sober. When he wasn't drinking, he was typically quiet; his natural personality introverted and insecure. He most likely turned to booze to feel confident. When he was sober, he'd be silly with us, tickling my ribs, or speaking in funny accents. One late night, I woke to a cockney accent in the kitchen, "By God, I think I will stick my pecker in the mashed potatoes." The sound of Mom, Roy and I chuckling echoed through the trailer.

Sometimes we'd gather together as a family and watch the World Wrestling Federation and Muhammad Ali boxing. My favorite was when he'd load us up in his old truck and take us to the drive-in movies. Roy and I would lay on a blanket outside on the ground eating popcorn, while Mom and Dad would sit close together in the cab, like two lovebirds on a date. We'd watch, "Butch Cassidy and The Sundance Kid", "The Good, the Bad and the Ugly" with Clint Eastwood." Or his all-time favorite, "True Grit", with John Wayne. I fell in love with the 'Wild West' watching Westerns with my dad. Unfortunately for all of us, these experiences were always short-lived.

This time, Dad arrived like a freight train, barreling through the tranquil routine we'd settled into, replacing it with his signature form of chaos. He swooped in and changed everything, linking arms with Mom, ready to run a 'tight ship.' This time, it was as if Mom and Dad were committed to showing us how united they were, and much of that centered on how they'd *handle* Roy and me. Together, they created a set of rules that we'd follow, otherwise we'd be punished.

One day, Roy and I came home from school together, which was becoming increasingly rare as Roy spent more and more time away from home with friends. Dad sat at the table sipping sweet tea while Mom stood at the stove frying liver and onions.

"Jana Lee," Mom called out, "will you check the mail?"

"Why?" I replied.

"What the sam-hill did you just say?"

"I said, *why*?" Then I caught myself. "I mean, yes ma'am."

"That's it." Mom threw the rag she was holding onto the counter. "Get your smart-ass in the bedroom, now."

I gave Roy a mournful look as I hung up my backpack and walked toward my bedroom. Mom walked in behind me and picked up a belt from the closet. "Bend over and pull your pants down," she said.

I pressed my lips together as I leaned over the bed. My bare bottom exposed, a combination of humiliation and anger rose inside of me. During these whippings I would go far away in my mind, leaving my body to take the pain of the lashes. She pulled her arm back and whipped the belt hard on my bare bottom three times. She'd say, "be still. If you move, you're gonna get more."

*Whack!*

*Whack!*

*Whack!*

I laid perfectly still.

"You know this hurts me more than it hurts you, but I will not tolerate disrespect."

"Yes, ma'am," I replied.

"Okay, now go clean yourself up for dinner."

"Yes, ma'am."

I wanted to puke. My heart was closed.

All I could think was: *I don't respect you.*

Things continued this way for months. Being younger than Roy, I didn't have a choice but to stay in the trailer most nights with Mom and Dad, treading lightly so I wouldn't rock the boat. During this stretch of time, I remember romancing suicide. I considered stealing my mom's bottle of Valium and taking it all. I played the scene out in my mind; Mom would find me, and wail over my lifeless body, feeling regret and sorrow for all the pain she had inflicted.

One cool Fall evening, Dad screeched into the driveway, stumbled inside, ambled to the kitchen and settled at the table ready to be served. Mom placed a heaping portion of chicken and dumplings in front of him. Dad was back on the bottle and had been drinking all day. His eyes were glassy, his body was swaying slightly, and his cheeks were bright red.

The food was cold.

Dad sneered.

Right on cue, Dad gripped the flimsy folding table and, in one motion, flipped it over, sending everything shattering to the floor. Dad chased after Mom, reached out, and caught her by the hair. Mom shrieked as Dad threw her to the ground. She screamed, "Archie, stop! I'm sorry!"

I wanted to call out—to scream for him to stop, but nothing came. It wouldn't have mattered anyway. I took off running, bolted out the door and onto the front lawn. That's when I began wringing my hands, praying to God to save me.

*Eyes closed.*

*Drifting.*

*Galaxies.*
*Nebulas.*
*Cradled in His arms.*
*It didn't matter who I was.*
*It didn't matter what I did.*
*It didn't matter what I believed.*
*It didn't matter how I worshipped.*
*It didn't matter what I worshipped.*
*There was infinite safety.*
*Total acceptance.*
*Pure, unwavering love.*

After what felt like a lifetime, I became aware once again of Dad cussing and throwing chairs against the walls as Mom wailed like a wounded animal. But I wasn't afraid. My body softened and relaxed. I looked up at the dark sky and let out a sigh. I had been there—to a blissful place, to Heaven, and I would never be the same again. Something had changed; I was no longer bound to these people who had given me life.

Once Dad sped off, I returned to the trailer to find Mom curled into a ball on the floor. I pulled her up and held her close. Now, at twelve, my body felt more mature, a closer physical match to my mom. I could bear her weight as she stood, then collapsed into me. Her eyes were swollen, her lip split wide open, her face mangled.

*Thank God*, I thought.

*Thank God I now know that you really do exist and that your love is unconditional—never ending.*

*They are not my parents.*

*You are.*

The following weekend, I returned to Sunday school at Hopewell Baptist Church. I was still basking in the glorious feeling of being held by the

Divine. The love I felt in the presence of Spirit was pure and penetrating; it was all-encompassing and true. It was not dependent on how much money I had, what religion I practiced, or how well I worshiped. Spirit didn't care whether I was Christian or not. I was loved unconditionally.

That morning in Sunday school, I sat in my hardwood chair and stared at the chalk board, which was covered in Bible verses. We were meant to copy them down and memorize them. I tried to settle into the work—yet I knew that none of it mattered.

As the Sunday school teacher pointed at the board and began to review each scripture, I raised my hand. "Mrs. Grey?"

"Yes, Jana Lee? She responded.

"I talked to God, and he told me that you don't have to be Christian to go to Heaven."

"What do you mean?" Mrs. Grey asked, her brow scrunched.

"Heaven is within each of us. God loves all of His creation and doesn't judge like humans do," I said, excitedly.

"Okay, young lady, it's time to stop this. Let's get back to work," she replied.

"Ma'am, I talked to Him. If someone doesn't know all these verses or even about Jesus at all, it's not an eternal sentence to Hell!"

Mrs. Grey's eyes narrowed. She stomped toward me, grabbed me by the arm, and led me into the hallway. She leaned close to my face, and through clenched teeth, she spat, "Jana Lee, what you just said is blasphemy. If you're listening to the voice of the devil, you are not welcome here."

"Not *welcome* here?" I asked confused.

Mrs. Grey folded her arms and tapped her foot, motioning toward the door. Feeling dejected, I turned and made my way out of the church into the blazing heat. I began the two-mile walk back home through the groves, breathing in the sweet fragrance of orange blossoms.

"God, why did that happen? Why would she—" my voice broke as sobs rose from my chest. I wanted to run back to the church, to force them to listen, to tell them about the infinite love I knew was out there. I wanted to help them see the truth because I knew that's what I had discovered.

*That is not your life.*

*This is.*

I drew a breath. Something inside me shifted. There was something about me—about everyone—that was Divine. The veil between my humanity and my Divinity was lifting.

The religion of my childhood, imprisoned me with dogma and doctrine from a constricted state of consciousness called fear. I was being taught that I was a sinner, that I was going to burn in hell if I wasn't perfect. I learned early through the gift of my trauma, that fear is the opposite of faith. By calling into question the fear-based teachings of the church, my faith in my direct connection to Spiritual guidance solidified. What religious beliefs were handed down to you that you're afraid to question?

*Chapter 18*

## SOUL SLAP
### ～ *1977* ～

Months later, Mom's bruises were barely healed from another one of the many violent lashings she believed she deserved. I sat on the couch watching TV while she and Dad ate dinner— her purple fingers wrapped around his hand. I felt sick, a voice inside me screaming as I listened to Mom giggle, swatting Dad's shoulder while he kissed her cheek. I was repulsed as he took his napkin and brushed a crumb off her face. Her eyelids and cheeks were purple. Her lip split, with a soft, yellow-white scab forming. Yet there they were, acting like newlyweds. It felt like I was watching a play—on the stage, two people acting out what they believed a real relationship looked like.

Dad took a swig of beer before tucking Mom's hair behind her ear and kissing her on the lips. I glanced over. He looked into her eyes and said, "I love you."

Before I could think, I shouted, "Ya'll make me sick!"

Their heads turned in unison just as I jumped up from the couch. "You pretend you're a happy couple, but Dad, you *beat* Mom!"

Mom gasped.

Dad's eyes narrowed.

"And you, Mom! You let him come back again and again to do it over and over! It's disgusting, I'm sick of you both—"

Just as the words left my mouth, Dad stood, shoving his chair back. He picked up the folding table and threw it up in the air, letting out a monstrous roar as it crashed to the floor. I stood my ground as he lunged forward and picked me up by my shoulders. He then tossed me like a rag-doll across the room, sending me crashing into the coffee table. I landed on my knees and skidded across the floor. As Dad kicked furniture out of the way, I looked down to see blood spurting out of my knees. Mom ran toward me, ducked under Dad, and yanked me to my feet. The door slammed behind us as Mom rushed me to the car and started the engine.

That was the first time Dad ever hit me.

*It would also be the last.*

As much pain as I was in, I felt empowered having finally spoken the truth.

Something ignited in me that night. I call it my 'inner-dragon slayer'.

I owned my voice and called them out on their hypocrisy and bullshit. I call that a 'soul slap'.

After getting bandages from the drugstore, we waited a while before heading home, hoping Dad would be gone when we got there. We drove past the trailer twice with the headlights switched off before finally pulling into our driveway. Noticing Dad's truck was gone, we felt safe to go back inside. The night was eerily still and silent. Mom took a deep breath and turned the knob, the light illuminating her bruised, battered face as we walked through the door. The floor was littered with broken furniture, shattered plates, shards of glass, and shredded books, the pages strewn from wall to wall. I walked straight to the kitchen, picked up the broom and started cleaning. I was on autopilot, only aware what I was doing when I bent down to pick up the dustpan from the floor. Blood dripped from under the bandage, reminding me of my situation. Mom sank into the couch and put her head in her hands. Instead of comforting her like I usually did, I continued to clean in silence, working to turn the chaos back into order.

Eventually, Mom stood, steadied herself, and made her way toward the bedroom. She sniffled softly as she closed the door, leaving me to finish cleaning in the lamplight. My knees ached, but I didn't care. I wanted everything back in its place. It turned out, Mom did too.

It was as if seeing Dad lay his hands on me was the wakeup call Mom needed. She never imagined he would be violent with his precious *'Time.'* With that newfound awareness came so much clarity. She began to understand that being in love with Archie Davis just because he was the father of her children and had been by her side since childhood was just a *story*. She'd learned in the hospital that her practiced thoughts became her beliefs, which created her reality. So, she began to repeat the thought *I am not in love with him*, hundreds of times each day. She did this until her feelings toward him yellowed, then turned an ashy shade of grey. She rewired her brain by creating this new narrative and repeating it consistently, until one day that thought took root and became her new reality.

*She was not in love with Archie Davis anymore.*

*She would never allow him back.*

When we are conditioned in childhood to 'never talk back' to adults, it teaches us not to trust our intuition. If we don't have emotionally intelligent parents who encourage us to advocate and speak up for ourselves then we become 'people pleasers'. People pleasers are caretakers – always putting others needs before their own. To grow into self-advocacy, we must learn to speak up and use our voice to set boundaries and ultimately to bring awareness to what doesn't serve us. Where in your life presently are you afraid to use your voice?

## Chapter 19

# FAMILIARITY
### ∽ 1981 ∽

"You're not standing the right way—you want to be able to throw your weight into it like this." Mom drew her arm back and brought it forward, demonstrating the perfect punch. Ok, like this?" I asked, miming what she had just done.

"Kinda," Roy interjected, "but you've gotta pull your arm back pretty far and hold your fist tight."

I drew my elbow back and threw one more punch, cutting the air with my fist.

"Almost perfect," Mom said, patting me on the shoulder. "Just keep practicing."

I was dripping with sweat. My arm was sore, my hips strained from the lessons I'd done with Roy and Mom for the past few days. The last thing I wanted to do was fight, but I didn't have a choice. Mom didn't give me a choice.

A few months earlier, on another painfully hot day hovering in the high 90's, my clothes stung as they lay against my skin. It was miserable with no air-conditioning in the trailer. Mom was in the front yard, watering the flowers by hand with the hose, doing her best to keep the plants alive through the summer heat. I had just hung up the phone with Tina, a classmate of Roy's, calling her a *slut* because she was bragging about screwing more guys than she could count. After placing the phone back on the wall, I headed outside to talk to Mom. Minutes later Tina was tearing through the middle of our yard in her Ford Mustang. She jerked the car into park, the engine still running. Tina lunged out the door running directly toward me, her face red with anger, her mouth clenched. She grabbed my head, jerking my hair with her left hand and repeatedly hitting me with her right hand, moving like a boxer on a speed bag. Mom dropped the hose and came closer. Instead of coming to help me, she just stood nearby and yelled at me to fight back. She didn't even try to get Tina to stop. Roy, hearing the ruckus from his room, came flying out the screen door and pulled Tina off me.

"You either need to learn to keep your mouth shut or learn how to fight. You're abrasive and bossy and your mouth gets you in trouble. "You're just like the Davis'," Mom spat her go-to insult.

Because of my insecurities, I compensated by spreading rumors about the girls I didn't like at school, recognizing their weak spots and exposing them. The girls hated my innate ability to read their behavior and constantly ganged up on me. Although I had a couple of very close girlfriends from middle school, Tammy and Lori, I often felt isolated and alone. I guess I shouldn't have been surprised when rumors began to circulate that there would be a fight on Saturday night at Mike Samson Ballpark—some girls were going to 'kick my ass.'

"I don't want to do this," I pleaded.

"Well, you have to," Mom said, "remember what happened with Tina," adjusting her oversize sunglasses while making the turn into the parking lot of the ballpark. "If you don't do this, they'll never leave you alone."

I stared out the window at the crowd of kids who had gathered, waiting to see what was about to happen. My heart was beating so fast and loud, it was deafening. I squinted my eyes and picked out the girl I knew was the ringleader. My best friend, Tammy came over and said, "Jana, I've got your back, you can do this." I stepped out of the car, walked up to her, pulled my arm back, and swung.

*Crack!*

My fist hit her face so hard that she instantly fell to the ground dazed. Without a word, I walked back to the car, shaking out my hand. My body began trembling uncontrollably. I hated my life. I didn't want to fight, my entire life felt like a fight.

"You did it!" Mom exclaimed as she peeled out of the parking lot.

"That was awesome!" Roy said, leaning forward in his seat.

"Now they'll never bother you again—trust me," Mom said with a grin.

I held the joint between my fingers and took a long drag. I looked up at the dark night sky, letting my mind drift.

*A beautiful house.*

*Brightly colored window boxes filled with lush flowers.*

*Big vacations.*

*Wealth.*

*Affluence.*

I listened to the soft tapping of leaves rubbing together in the breeze. My body felt deliciously heavy, my thoughts slow and purposeful. Cannabis had become one of my favorite tools to cope with life. When I was high, I was able to be the observer of my experience and create some distance from the insanity of my life. I would walk through the halls of school acutely aware that I was only experiencing a small part of reality. The out-of-body experience I had at age twelve set the stage for me to remember who I really am—a *soul*. I was becoming aware that all experiences were transient, ephemeral, and fleeting. This allowed me to cope with the constant stress of living in Plant City. When I was high, I'd linger in my daydreams as long as I could, my mind traveling every inch of the future I intended.

I started to feel the effects of the joint wearing off, I looked down at my watch. Noticing it was almost 9:30 pm, I stood up from the lawn chair and took off running toward the trailer. Mack's car was already parked outside, and he was standing in the driveway. I held my breath and braced for his reaction.

"What the fuck, Jana? We're late for the party," he called out.

"I'm sorry, I lost track of time!" I said, trying to sound cheery.

"Get in the goddamn car," he barked.

I opened the door and got into the passenger seat as he sat down hard in his seat and slammed the door behind him. "I don't know what the fuck is wrong with you, but you kept me waiting for a half hour. What were you doing out there?"

"Nothing, I—"

"Oh *nooooothing*?" he mocked.

"Nothing, I just smoked a joint and lost track of time."

"You're a dumb bitch, you know that?"

I couldn't muster another word. My heart dropped, I hated when he spoke to me that way.

Mack and I had gotten into a relationship a year prior. Four years older than me, Mack was popular and incredibly handsome. He had olive skin, bright green eyes, disarming dimples, and brown curly hair. One summer day, while swimming at Lithia Springs, we caught each other's glance. The chemistry was intense. I had never felt such an instant physical attraction. Walking to the concession stand, he pulled me behind the building, leaned forward, brushed the hair out of my face, and kissed me.

I was head over heels. Only weeks before my fifteenth birthday, I gave Mack my most valuable possession: my virginity. It wasn't some beautiful experience like I had dreamed it would be. He was drunk; it was painful; I bled heavily. That night, he took me home in silence. After that, I knew I *had* to make it work with Mack long term, otherwise, it would mean I was a slut.

At first, our relationship was good. We had fun together. He took me to Daytona Beach for spring break; we went to keg parties and concerts. He became the center of my world.

But as time wore on, Mack's layers were peeled back. He had a temper, he could be irritable, disrespectful, and downright abusive. He was dealing coke. He cheated on me constantly, belittled me in front of friends, humiliating me when he had the chance. Sometimes I fought back, but most of the time I stood there and took it, because something inside me forced me to stay.

*Familiarity.*

When we arrived at the party, there were already dozens of cars parked around a huge bonfire that lit the sprawling field. Mack got out of the car without a word, slamming the door behind him. I slowly slid out after him and made my way to the keg. As I filled my cup with beer, Mack walked up to a group of girls and put his arm around one of them. It was Tina. I felt nauseous as I watched him, wishing things were different. Wishing *he* was different. But he wasn't. He took her by the hand and led her away. I could hear her laughing as they disappeared into the woods.

After fifteen minutes had passed, my anxiety and anger were at all-time highs. I threw my beer to the ground and stomped in their direction. As I approached the wooded area, Mack and Tina were scrambling out from under the dense branches, Mack still fiddling with his zipper.

"What the fuck are you doing?" I screamed, shoving him as hard as I could.

"What am *I* doing? What the fuck are *you* doing?" He screamed back, his face now inches from mine.

"What were ya'll doing?" I asked, as if I didn't know.

"Get the fuck away from me!" he yelled, shoving me back as Tina flung her cup of Crown Royal in my face. I was momentarily blinded from the sting of the whiskey and quickly grabbed my face, wiping my eyes with my shirt. They walked away chatting as if nothing had happened.

I found a spot a short distance from the frenzy of the party to sit on the cool dirt and cry. It wasn't long before Mack found me, intent on terrorizing me some more. He was carrying a chainsaw and brought it close to my face before pulling the starting cord. The engine sputtered but didn't start. I leapt to my feet and ran, Mack right behind me, continuing to pull the cord. A small group nearby stopped what they were doing and stared in disbelief, some in shock and fear, others laughing at the ridiculousness of the scene.

When he caught up to me, he grabbed my arm and dragged me to his car. He opened the door and shoved me into the passenger side. He quickly moved around the front of the car, slamming his weight into the driver's seat, never taking his eyes off me. Furious, he began shouting nonsense, screaming insults, calling me a bitch and a whore. Before I could say anything back, he lifted his arm.

*Smack!*

I lost my breath as his open hand crossed my face. Sobbing, I ran from the car holding my cheek. He chased after me, begging and pleading, but there was nothing he could do. Cheating on me was one thing, screaming at me was another, now he'd done the unthinkable...

He'd turned me into my mother.

*Chapter 20*

# CHRISTMAS DREAMS
## ⌒ *1982* ⌒

The soft sounds of electric guitar riffs drifted from Roy's bedroom. He'd been in there all day, practicing Tom Petty songs on the early Christmas present Mom had given him the day before. Roy had been wanting a guitar for years and Mom had finally been able to afford it because the music shop offered a layaway plan. Now, having a full day of practice under his belt, he was starting to get the hang of it. I sat in the living room half-listening to Roy and staring at the twinkling lights, marveling at the magical ambiance they brought to our sad little trailer.

Earlier that week, I'd started to entertain an idea that surprised me. It began as a fleeting thought—something I could easily push away. Regardless of the steady diet of heartbreak, grief and sorrow my dad consistently fed me, I still loved him. It was obviously a skewed view of love. I wished for the best version of my daddy, dreaming he could show up one day and make all the pain of the past disappear. As I blew out the candles on my seventeenth birthday cake, I found myself wishing that things could be different with Dad. I hadn't seen him in so long, I imagined him down and out with nothing to live for. I could hear his voice in my head, "Poor ole Poppa, nobody loves me." I hated to think of the approaching holiday and imagine him alone. I pictured him sitting in a bar somewhere drinking to feel whole, or spending the night alone, passed out in his truck. It wasn't long before I began to feel it: the familiar heartache. I'd lay in bed and, in my mind, replay the moments when he was at his best. I'd recall jumping into his arms and hugging him tight or resting my head on his shoulder while we watched Western movies. I thought of the tender moments we shared; the sweet pet names he had for me and his low, raspy voice as he sang to me:

*Your time hasn't come yet baby*
*You got a few dreams to go*
*Your time hasn't come yet baby*
*When it does your heart will know*[9]

Although most of my time was spent imagining my future, adventuring to far-flung places, and envisioning all the success in the world, a small part of me could get caught up in the pain of missing my dad. Most of the time, that pain was manageable. It was a part of me that I rarely acknowledged—like a cut that's long-since scarred.

With Christmas just four days away, I'd spend time imagining Dad with us as we filled our plates with turkey and all the fixin's. I pictured him humming along to the Elvis Christmas album we'd play from morning until nightfall. The thing is, I knew the truth about Dad in my guts. How could I not? But something inside me found a tiny shred of hope, grasped it, and refused to let it go. My role as caretaker was firmly in place. I knew we could never be a family, but I wished for the love I believed only my daddy could provide. I just couldn't let my dad spend Christmas alone.

I started by casually asking Mom if he could come to dinner. "Please, Mom? Can he?" I pleaded, my eyes wide.

"Are you kidding, Jana Lee Davis? No, he's not coming here."

"Please?"

"Absolutely not. You know as well as I do that this isn't a good idea.

---

9 Elvis Presley, "Your Time Hasn't Come Yet Baby", Speedway (1968)

No good can come of him being here."

"Pleeeeeeeease?" I begged.

"Not a chance," she said firmly.

It went on like this for a couple of days. I nagged her over breakfast, while I got ready for school, while I begrudgingly did my homework, before I went out, and after I came home. Out of sheer desperation for me to stop, she gave in. "Listen. I'm going on a date on Christmas Eve. Dad can come by while I'm gone, but that's it. He can't stay any longer. Okay?"

"Yes, yes, okay! Thank you, Momma! Thank you!" I squealed.

On Christmas Eve, Roy played his guitar as I straightened the ornaments on the tree, made sure the lights were hanging right, and neatened up the living room. Around 7 pm, Dad's 1956, fully restored, red Ford F-100, rumbled into the driveway.

I ran out the door, jogged to his car, and jumped into his arms. "Daddy! Merry Christmas!" I yelled.

"Time!" He replied, hugging me tight. That's when I noticed it. A strong odor of liquor.

*Oh God, what have I done?*

"Where's yo mammy?" he slurred.

I pictured Mom out on her date, flipping her hair as she laughed. I imagined her nodding intently as the man stared deeply into her beautiful golden-green eyes and smiled. I pictured her ashing her cigarette, then taking a drag during a pause in the conversation.

"She's just out doing some last-minute shopping," I said.

He narrowed his eyes, grabbed the open bottle of whiskey from his truck, and stomped into the trailer. "Hey Duke! Where's yo mammy!?" he called out.

Roy came out of his bedroom and responded, "She's out."

Dad took a long slug from the bottle, then wiped his mouth on his sleeve. "Sh'better be back soon."

Dad barely spoke a word as Roy and I went about our business. For a little while, I tried to engage him in conversation, but he wanted no part of talking to me. The only words he spoke were about Mom, what a whore she was, and the disgusting things she was probably doing with some other guy. His energy was tense—it felt scary—just like it used to.

The more he talked, the more nervous I became that Mom would come back while Dad was still there. I went to the kitchen and pulled the telephone cord into the laundry room, closed the door, trying to reach Mom at the restaurant. I knew that when she got home, Dad would take one look at her and know she had been on a date. She couldn't come home, not with Dad drunk and spewing filth about her. I tried everything I could think of to warn her, but it was too late. Just as I hung up the phone for the very last time and went to my bedroom, headlights flashed in the driveway.

I knew with all my being that she should not come inside. I tiptoed across my room and quickly made my way out the window. The cool, dry night air hit my face as I bolted to the driver's side door to warn her. I flung the door open as she gathered her purse.

"Please, don't go inside. He's here and he's drunk, it's gonna be trouble," I said panicking, shifting my weight from foot to foot.

"I knew he'd be trouble. But don't be silly, I'm not sitting in my car until he leaves," she replied defiantly, stepping out of the car.

"He's been asking where you are since he got here. Please, don't go inside Mom," I begged, placing my hands on her shoulders.

She laughed, shaking my hands off. She then straightened her dress and walked toward the trailer with me following close behind. Just as she stepped through the back door, Dad called out, "Where the fuck you been, whore?" In one swift move, he yanked the phone off its place on the kitchen wall. Mom didn't have a moment to react before Dad pulled his arm back and smashed the phone down across the left side of her face. She fell to the ground, her face instantly swelling, blood spurting from her temple. She let out a shriek and brought her hands to her face. I stood in shock, waiting for her to curl into a ball, but instead of lying there lifeless like she usually did, she scrambled to her feet and bolted to her room.

Roy stomped into the kitchen shouting, "You better get the hell outta here!"

Dad's eyes narrowed as he ran after Roy, but Roy was too fast, escaping out the front door. Unable to catch him, Dad turned his attention to the new guitar. He raised it high over his head and forcefully slammed it against the wall, splintering Roy's prized possession into hundreds of pieces. He wasn't finished. He went back to Roy's room a second time, grabbed his amp and brought it into the living room. He threw it on the ground and began stomping on the speaker. His eyes were bloodshot, his gaze vacant.

Just then, Mom pulled open the door of her bedroom. Her face was so swollen that her left eye would no longer open. She was holding her .22 pistol.

"Get the hell out of my house!" she shouted, raising the gun.

"Whatchu gonna do? You gon shoot me?" Dad slurred.

Mom steadied herself. Blood streaming down her face.

"I'd like ta see ya try!" he shouted, then drained the last of the whiskey with two loud gulps and one loud belch. Noticing it was empty, he hurled the bottle at the mirror that hung on the far wall. The bottle hit the mirror with such force that it went right through the glass, penetrating the flimsy wood paneling behind the mirror: the bottle remaining intact.

There was an instant of silence before Mom ran toward Dad with the gun, forcing him out the door onto the lawn. I crawled out of my bedroom window again, this time running to a nearby neighbor's house. I banged on the door rapidly. My neighbor yelled out, "go away, we don't want your family's drama!"

"Please call the police, my mom is shooting my dad," I begged.

They let me inside and allowed me to use their phone to call 9-11. Certain the police would be there soon, I stood at the window with my frightened neighbors watching Dad run across the lawn. Mom right behind him, firing the pistol again and again in his direction. As the third shot rang out, he fell to the ground, writhing in pain.

While Dad lay bleeding in the grass, Roy grabbed a shovel. He ran over to Dad's truck and began beating it relentlessly. Mom stood dazed, in shock still clutching the gun, watching as Dad hobbled to the neighbors across the street.

By the time police cars lit up the property, Dad's truck was mangled. Because it was Christmas Eve, a night when domestic violence calls skyrocket, there was only one ambulance available, and we had to share it with Dad. While the EMT tended to Dad's gunshot wound in the back, Mom and I sat in the front, next to the driver. Still in her beautiful date clothes, Mom looked like the bride of Frankenstein. Her face was grotesque—so swollen that it seemed like her head had doubled in size. My heart fell, and guilt bubbled up inside me. She allowed Dad back for me this time and look how it ended.

I stared through the windshield. I felt exhausted, but a different kind of exhausted. It was the feeling of being tired down to my bones. I should have known better than to entertain the idea that Dad could be around us without wreaking havoc. He wasn't capable of a healthy relationship, and when Mom, Roy, and I were around him, we were sucked back into the sick spiral too.

Right then and there, I made a vow. I would no longer have a relationship with my dad. I needed to find other ways to fill the void he'd left. Instead of wishing things would be better, I settled on the inevitable truth. If I wanted a better life, I needed to create it. I didn't just need to get out of that trailer, I needed to get away from Plant City altogether.

# Chapter 21

## STRAWBERRY QUEEN
### ∽ *1984* ∼

I stood backstage and stared at my reflection and practiced smiling. My chocolate brown eyes, my small smile filled with silver metal. Granny had finally paid for me to get braces my junior year. I couldn't bear the thought of smiling on stage, but it seemed there was no choice. It was almost time for the Strawberry Queen pageant to begin. I touched up my eye shadow, swept more blush on my cheeks, then scurried over to join a group of girls gathering in the wings.

Now in my senior year of high school, with Dad and Mack out of the picture, life was improving. I was starting to make headway on my dream to get out of Plant City, buckling down, studying hard and getting better grades. I was also making friends with girls who were more like me; girls with dreams and aspirations, girls with ambition. Life was coming together for me in ways it never seemed to before. I was comparing myself less and feeling more confident.

I nervously tapped my foot as girls' names were called one by one. By the time they called my name, I'd made myself so uptight, worrying I might trip and fall. I walked slowly and purposefully through the curtains onto the stage as the host introduced me: "Next up, is Jana Lee Davis, everybody!"

The crowd applauded. Granny and Mom waved from their seats in the front row.

I crossed the stage, twirling in my dress on both corners as the host continued, "Her favorite subject in school is social studies and she loves fashion."

I took my place next to the host. The spotlight lit his polyester suit and bright, striped tie. He looked at me, then back at the crowd with a huge smile and asked, "So, Jana, what are your dreams for the future?"

My heart raced as my mind went completely blank. The crowd was silent; the microphone squealed. I opened my mouth to say something about attending college, but the only thing that came out was, ". . . oh shit."

The crowd gasped. Mom stifled a laugh as Granny sat with her mouth wide open. I was politely ushered off the stage. I was eliminated immediately, dashing my hopes of becoming Strawberry Queen. Feeling the disappointment, I slumped against the wall backstage, my braces cutting into the sides of my cheeks. I walked over to the mirror, grabbed a tissue, and began rubbing the makeup off my face until my cheeks were raw.

That night, I lay on my bed with a *Cosmopolitan* magazine spread across my lap. It had become a constant battle with Mom who refused to pay for my subscriptions: I kept sending the cards off anyway. *Cosmopolitan* had everything: Fashion, sex, celebrities; snippets of the life I so desperately desired. Reading the magazine word-for-word and staring at the photos became one of my favorite things to do—it was how I spent nearly all my free time. I was particularly fascinated by the models in each perfectly styled photo. I wanted to know everything about them and the magical lives they led.

Lately, it seemed that Costa Rica was the playground for models and celebrities alike. The magazine was filled with photos of models running on pristine beaches, playing volleyball, sunning themselves on the shore, or splashing in the turquoise surf. Costa Rica became a setting for the coming attractions I was imagining for my life. I'd spend hours lost in daydreams that were so real, I could feel my feet traipsing through white sand and hear the sound of the surf lapping at the shore. Snuggling into bed, I'd revel in dreams about traveling and experiencing the world. Little did I know at the time, I was in the active process of creating my future.

One night, I sat in my bedroom flipping through a recent issue of *Cosmopolitan* with a pile of older issues at my feet. That's when I heard a knock at the front door.

"It's open!" Mom called out.

"Janice! Get out here!" It was Buddy Graves. He was with his friend, Phillip, who I'd also known all my life.

I continued to read with one ear on the conversation happening in the living room, "What's going on?" Mom asked.

"I've got big news for you!" Buddy announced. "I won big on the Super Bowl. I mean BIG. $10,000 big."

"That's great, Buddy!" Mom responded.

"Yeah, and I want to take y'all somewhere to celebrate! Let's get you out of town for a bit! Anywhere you want!" "What?" she replied. "But where would we go?"

"Anywhere!" he said, his voice booming.

I flew out of my room, "Costa Rica! We *have* to go to Costa Rica!"

Buddy and Mom looked at me like I was insane.

"Costa Rica?" Mom asked.

"Yes, here! Look!" I ran into my bedroom and grabbed the Cosmopolitan I had been reading on my bed. I flipped through the pages until I reached the picture of a tall, svelte model jogging on white sand. "See?"

"Well, you've convinced *me*," Buddy said with a laugh.

"That does look beautiful." Mom smiled. "Is this real, Buddy? Are you sure about this?"

"Of course, I am. Let's get you ladies out of here."

At the time, there was conflict in Central America—the Contra War. Costa Rica bordered Nicaragua so, naturally, Mom and Buddy worried about our safety. Even though the idea seemed crazy, they decided to go for it without much discussion. Within the hour, we were packed and on the road in Buddy's van, making our way through the night to Miami. I was so excited I couldn't sleep. Instead, I stared out the window asking myself:

*Did my imagination make this happen?*

*If that was true, what else was possible?*

We arrived at the airport and excitedly ran to the ticket counter where Buddy paid for our tickets in cash. After making our way through security and to the gate, I sat nervously and watched the bags being loaded onto the aircraft. I hadn't been outside of Florida since I was four and I'd never been on an airplane. After the gate agent called us to board, I slid into my small, cramped seat next to Mom, buckled my seatbelt, and stared out the window. As we were racing down the tarmac, my body rumbled with the roar of the engine. Before I knew it, we took to the sky. I watched as the landscape slowly changed from swampy wetlands to the big blue ocean, then finally to mountains and rainforest.

As the plane eased onto the runway, I was vibrating with excitement. When we finally exited the plane, a blast of hot air slammed me in the face. The sky was bright blue and cloudless. It was the perfect welcome. I held the railing as we made our way down the portable staircase and onto the tarmac. We made our way through the confusing airport collecting our bags on the way. Buddy hailed a cab and somehow in 'Spanglish' communicated to the driver to take us to an upscale hotel. As the car zipped through busy streets, I was immediately taken by the size of the metropolis; I had no idea San Jose was such a massive city. The streets were buzzing with traffic, the walkways packed with people in cool, breezy clothes. In the distance, the driver pointed to Irazu Volcano jutting into the sky, flanked by smaller mountains and thick, lush rainforest.

When we arrived at the hotel, we were informed that it was election time in Costa Rica. That meant the city was packed—electric. Over the next few days, we enjoyed every luxury our hotel had to offer. We braved the crowds and ate out at beautiful local restaurants and spent the days exploring the far corners of the big city. We visited old churches, and shopped, Buddy paying for anything we wanted. I loaded up on tiny trinkets—the kind I coveted at Aunt Ginny's.

To get out of the city and see more of the country, the staff at the hotel recommended a bus tour to the volcano. On the drive, I observed extreme poverty that I hadn't seen at home. Children played barefoot in the dirt wearing rags. Makeshift shelters built from scraps served as homes. Roadside fruit stands with piles of fresh, tropical fruit begged for someone to stop and just buy *something*. I was poor, but being poor in central Florida looked a lot better than being poor in a third-world country. It expanded my awareness of our world.

One evening, we made our way through the throngs of people who chanted and waved flags, rallying for their candidate. Being a 'gringa' with blonde hair, I stood out like a sore thumb. The men marching through the city leered at me, some cat calling, and one man even reached out and grabbed my butt. Anger bubbled up inside me and I roared, "Get the hell off me!"

As the man moved away, I smiled to myself. My inner-dragon slayer was still there, lying in wait. I felt powerful, knowing I could access that part of myself.

On our last evening, the hotel concierge recommended the most famous seafood restaurant in San Jose. When we arrived, we heard voices inside, but the door was locked. Buddy wasn't deterred and pounded on the heavy wooden door, rattling the hinges. "We have 'dinero' and we're hungry," he announced with his Southern drawl.

A small man with a big smile cracked open the door. "Are you American?" he asked, in excellent English.

"We are," said Buddy. "We head back to the U.S. tomorrow and our hotel told us we couldn't miss this place before we left."

The owner opened the door fully, invited us inside, and led us to a table in the corner. The only other people in the restaurant were a large party, engaged in energetic conversation. Mom, who devoured news and was always up on current events, recognized the man at the head of the table immediately. When the waiter placed her tequila sunrise in front of her, she whispered in his ear. The waiter nodded. Then Mom stood up,

*Me, President Monge, Buddy Graves, First Lady, Mom*

raised her glass and said, "Salute el Presidente!" in a perfect accent. The man Mom recognized was Luis Alberto Monge, the leading candidate in the Presidential election.

Mr. Monge smiled and came over to the table, offering to take a photo with us. Elated, we gathered together, and Buddy handed the waiter his camera. We smiled as the flash went off. When we returned to our seats after more small talk with Mr. Monge, I let myself feel every ounce of the moment. Here I was, in Costa Rica, rubbing elbows with a foreign dignitary. Little ol' me, from Plant City, Florida, had dreamed, imagined and now manifested a moment like this. I thought back to nights spent with *Cosmopolitans* spread all over my bed, then shutting off my light, and traveling in my mind to this very place. And now, I had arrived. That's when I understood, my way of anesthetizing the pain of my childhood had become my most powerful tool—my imagination was orchestrating my life.

A week after our return, Mom and I sat in front of the television watching Barbara Walters interview the newly elected President of Costa Rica – Luis Alberto Monge.

Finally, my mom and I were living peacefully together my last year of high school. Roy was now out of the house on his own journey of self-discovery. During his last year of high school, he was headed down the wrong path and started using harder drugs. He spent days and nights out with friends partying until the morning. Mom was wearing thin; she couldn't control him, and their fights were intensifying. Then, as summer break neared, Roy got a girl pregnant. That was his wakeup call. Now, a father-to-be, he headed to Texas to be an evangelical missionary with a Pentecostal Church. He turned his life over to Jesus and became a born-again Christian. We didn't speak much after that, no more than a catch up here and there. Sometimes I missed the way we once were, how close we were as kids. But as we grew older, we also grew apart.

After the experiences in Miami and San Jose, I had fallen in love with the energy of big cities. I had never felt more alive than I did on that trip. I began to imagine myself living in Miami, attending school, and meeting interesting and influential people.

Granny's only sister to have an advanced degree, Aunt Bea, had attended Purdue University. Her husband was a radiologist and Aunt Bea made a name for herself in real estate in their hometown of Bloomfield Hills, Michigan. Granny would brag that her sister was neighbors with the former CEO of Chrysler Corp, Lee Iacocca. In our families' eyes, Aunt Bea had *arrived*. She was the symbol of great success in our extended family.

Aunt Bea had her eyes on me since the gun incident. She had reached out and attempted to take me to live with her while I was with Aunt Ginny. Since then, she would send me school supplies and would periodically call me to talk. During one such conversation on a Sunday afternoon, I twirled the phone cord around my finger as she asked, "So, what do you think you want to do after high school?"

"I haven't really told anyone this yet," I said. "But I'd love to be a fashion merchandiser, or maybe a professional makeup artist for movies."

"Those are great goals," Aunt Bea said enthusiastically. "So, what are you doing to make those things happen?"

"I'm not sure what the next step should be. My grades aren't the best, and I don't think I would do well on college placement tests. I found a specialty school in South Florida that I think might be ideal for me."

"That's great," she replied. "I can't wait to hear more about it! Tell me everything."

Aunt Bea listened as I excitedly shared all I knew about Bauder College in Ft. Lauderdale, a small fine arts school I had seen advertised in *Cosmopolitan*. She asked challenging questions and encouraged me to go for it. I found so much comfort and inspiration in her words. She was the first of many mentors and guides I attracted throughout my life.

Over the next few months, Aunt Bea and Granny helped me organize everything I needed to apply for low-income grants, so I'd be able to pay for tuition. With their guidance, I was finally on a path to get out of Plant City. I was accepted into Bauder College; frankly, it was the only place I attempted. I enrolled in Fashion Merchandising with dreams of being a professional buyer. I was on the path to achieving my dreams. The funny thing about dreams, however, is that they evolve as we evolve.

Perseverance is one of the greatest qualities you can develop to live the life of your dreams. Most people allow doubt to creep in, and they throw in the towel before they realize success. When you know who you are, and that knowingness is rooted in 'I am deserving of having a spectacular life' then you will have developed perseverance. What dream have you given up on? Now is the time to have a happy childhood.

*Chapter 22*

# GIRLS LIKE ME
## 1984

It was my first semester of college. I stared across the bar at a tall, muscular, handsome man. His green eyes glistened in the low light as he reached for his drink. I had seen him many times at Shooters, a waterfront bar on the Intercoastal Waterway in Ft. Lauderdale with luxury yachts of all sizes lining the dock. I couldn't stop staring at him, willing him to make eye contact with me. When he did, my heart began to race. Moments later, he came up from behind me, grabbed my waist and whispered in my ear, "Hey, beautiful." A shiver ran down my spine. He introduced himself, and shared he was a firefighter. He was so sexy, with a scruffy beard and sandy blonde hair. He reached out and grabbed my hand. I loved the way his felt; big and warm, dwarfing mine.

I finished my drink and excused myself to go to the bathroom. I stared in the mirror, giving myself a sly smile. I knew he was attracted to me, and I felt the same about him. Yet I was feeling insecure and was back in the pattern of comparing myself to the other girls at school. I gave myself a pep talk before returning.

Back at the bar, the firefighter tapped his glass against mine, which he had refilled when I was away from the table. We both drained our glasses quickly, as the music swelled, he leaned in and kissed me. He pulled me closer to him, becoming more and more passionate. That's when my eyes started feeling heavy.

Before I knew it, the room began to spin, and I was struggling to stand up. He held onto me and helped me outside to the valet. The last thing I remember was asking him to take me to my dorm. I was incoherent, coming in and out of consciousness.

*Stabbing Pain*
*Eyes open*
*His face in mine*
*His hands on my body*
*I shove at his chest*
*I can't push him off*

My body was limp beneath his. I wanted to scream—to run as fast as I could. I wanted to cry out for my mom, for Jesus, for anyone to save me. But I was powerless beneath him. My thoughts continued to swim as he pushed himself into me. I would become conscious, then pass out, then become conscious once more, until finally I was out.

The next morning, I woke to sounds of lawnmowers and cars whizzing past the open window. As soon as the light hit my eyes, pain shot through my head like a bullet through soft tissue. The pain was so intense, I could barely keep my eyes open for more than a moment.

*A shitty bed*
*Worn sheets*

"Let's go," he said in a vacant voice.

I dragged myself out of the bed and gathered my things before following him out the front door and into his car. I shifted uncomfortably in my clothes from the night before. The outfit I'd worked so hard to pick out now felt like a prison jumpsuit. We drove the ten minutes to my dorm in silence. I stared out the window watching all the normal people going about their days while I was trapped in my internal hell.

When we pulled up outside my building, I felt sick to my stomach. I slammed the car door and walked toward the dorm, stumbling over my feet. I quickly darted into my room, threw off my clothes, wrapped my body in a towel, and grabbed a bar of soap. Rushing to the bathroom to wash off the night, I pulled back the thin, plastic curtain and turned the knob, sending hot water cascading out of the faucet. I flung myself inside and scrubbed my body with the bar of soap until my skin nearly blistered. I needed to rid myself of his filth.

When I stepped out of the shower, I caught my reflection in the steamed-up mirror. "You make me sick!" I said aloud to myself. I was utterly disgusted by my own naivety. How could I have gotten myself into this horrible situation? I gathered my things from the bathroom, went to my room and pulled on a pair of shorts and a baggy tee-shirt. I tucked myself into bed lying in the fetal position and began to sob, thinking, *this is what happens to girls like me.*

It never occurred to me to call the police or tell anyone. I internalized that I deserved this somehow. My self-worth was so low, I didn't consider that I was a victim of a crime. I never wanted to be a victim. Victims are weak, my mom was weak, and I did not want to be like her.

Laying there on the bed, I knew I needed to change. I had to be strong and focused, or I might end up back in Plant City. The problem was, I didn't have the tools to make changes and I didn't know if I could do it by myself.

As the weeks passed after the night-long rape, I spiraled. Growing up, I didn't have healthy parents to teach me how to care for myself. I did what I saw my family do; I numbed my feelings. It was easy. The drinking age in Florida was eighteen and Ft. Lauderdale was known as 'Ft. Liquor-dale'.

Night after night, I went to clubs with friends, drinking until I couldn't feel anything. I'd dance and sing, flirting with any guy who would give me some small sliver of attention, frequently going home with them. I was incapable of allowing myself to sit in my discomfort for more than a second.

As time passed, my body felt awful. I wasn't doing anything to take care of myself. I'd spend nearly all the time when I wasn't partying in bed trying to recover. One day as I was napping, I bolted up in bed. I couldn't remember the last time I had my period. I tried thinking back, counting the days and weeks, but the last time I remembered having it was *before* I was raped. I ran to the nearest pharmacy, grabbed a pregnancy test, headed back to my dorm and took it in the bathroom. My mouth was dry, my head spinning with thoughts of what I would do if it was positive. And then the cross appeared.

*Pregnant.*

I sat on the toilet with my head in my hands. My heart was pounding in my chest. I couldn't believe that I had gotten myself into this situation. How could I have forgotten, even for a second, that I was White Trash Jana?

When I returned to my room, my roommates were at the table doing homework and chatting like any other day. The scene of normality, in contrast to what I was experiencing, only added to my self-loathing. I had to call my granny; she would know what to do. I picked up the phone and dialed, my hands shaking.

"Hello," she answered.

"Granny, I need help." I sputtered. I only shared that I was pregnant, not how, with whom or any of the gory details of my circumstances. She calmly instructed me to call a clinic and she would wire me the money through Western Union. After hanging up, I grabbed the phone book from a table nearby and squinted through tears to find the number of an abortion clinic. I knew I couldn't possibly take care of a baby. I was eighteen years-old and could barely take care of myself.

On the day of the abortion, I pulled my fine hair into a ponytail and made my way across town to the clinic. There, I sat in the waiting room surrounded by pregnant women, some balancing babies on their laps.

There were other girls like me with swollen, sad eyes, holding back tears.

"Jana Davis?" a nurse called.

My heart pounded.

"Jana Davis?"

I wished I was at Granny's, lying next to her, as she lovingly stroked my hair and told me how much she loved me. But I was here by myself, and it was time.

In the exam room, I laid my clothes on a chair in the corner of the cold, stark room, put on a hospital gown, and climbed on the table as instructed. After talking through the procedure with the doctor, he asked, "Are you ready?"

"No," I whispered silently to myself.

With that, the procedure began. I closed my eyes as I felt myself pinched and pulled, tugged, then vacuumed out. I wanted to vomit. I wanted to scream. But there was no point.

*This is what happens to girls like me.*

## Chapter 23

# THE TIDES TURN

### ✑ *1985* ✑

Following the abortion, my body was showing the signs of my consistent, unhealthy behavior. Between my grief and the constant stress, there was little to no relief. Still wishing to drown out my feelings, I went out clubbing nearly every single night, letting myself live the glory of the Fort Lauderdale party scene. I was dealing with painful bouts of strep throat and nearly constant conjunctivitis. My body was manifesting my inability to speak up and advocate for myself and reminding me there was so much of myself I didn't want to see. I was internally at war. It seemed that, as an eighteen-year-old, raised in my family, I just wasn't mature enough to handle living on my own.

I thought about Mom. Since she'd pushed Dad out of her life once and for all, my relationship with her had improved. She was soft and kind, willing to focus on me, helping me through as much as she possibly could. It was as if she were trying to make up for the past, finally caring for herself, which gave her extra energy to care for me too. Now nearly an adult, I finally felt like I had the parent I'd always wanted and needed. It was time to call on her.

I stood at a payphone, waiting nervously for the operator to connect the collect call. I pressed the receiver to my ear. Tears pricked the back of my eyes when I heard her voice: "Hello?"

"Mom, can you come here?" I sniffed.

"Honey, are you okay?" Mom asked.

"No, I think I need you." I placed my hand on the payphone box and rested my head on the wall.

"What's going on?" she asked. I could picture her face; she was worried.

"Things are just hard—I'm always sick. I feel. . .sad, almost all the time."

"Oh, Jana Lee. Do you want to come home?"

"I will never go back to Plant City!" I said, closing my eyes.

"What can I do?" she asked.

"I need you, Mom. Please."

"Of course, Honey. I'll find a way to get there as soon as possible. Until then, try to relax, okay?"

It started with a visit. Mom made the four-hour trip to Ft. Lauderdale and brought cleaning supplies to get my room back in order and food to pack the small fridge in my dorm room. She took one look at me and knew that one visit wouldn't be enough. I was struggling to keep it together.

Within the next month, Mom sold the trailer and land in Turkey Creek and moved to Ft. Lauderdale to be with me. We found a new apartment and moved in; it was close enough I could walk to class.

Mom began working at the Spaghetti Warehouse as a bartender. She loved the job and became super social with her younger coworkers who loved how wise and caring Mom was. At home, she was a calm, steady presence and, with her, I stabilized.

Mom and I found a groove that was comfortable. We'd both wake up early and have coffee together at the kitchen table. We'd then go off to our respective activities for the day, finally seeing one another again in the evening. Though I still went to parties and slept with men sometimes, I found myself in a space where I was able to discern when it was too much.

I would pump the breaks when things started to feel out of control. It was the healthiest I'd been since moving away from Plant City.

With things on a better path, I loved spending time with Mom. This was her chance to support me in my dreams by providing the stability she couldn't when we were in Plant City. With her love, praise and constant presence, I was feeling stronger—better able to support myself.

One night, we sat on the couch together, me with a textbook and Mom with a novel, both reading in the lamplight. I looked over at Mom, smiling to myself seeing her in this new home with me, so different, but also the same. I loved watching her read to herself. My favorites were her soft smiles at romantic scenes, and scowls during the drama. I liked to imagine her head swimming with words, brimming at the edges with characters brought to life.

"Mom," I said. "You know, you saved my life."

She closed her book and looked intently back at me, "Well, Honey, you've saved mine more than once."

"I love you," I said, reaching my hand out and touching her foot.

"I love you too, Precious. Listen." She put her book down and inched closer to me. "I don't want you to be like me. I don't want you to depend on a man. I want you to be an independent woman. I know I haven't modeled that to you, but I see you now, working hard and studying, and I'm so proud of you."

"It's hard sometimes," I said, biting my lip.

"I know it is, Honey. But you're a 'can do' girl."

I looked over, my eyes meeting hers, and the deepest wellspring of love flooded my body.

After two years of school, I had finally hit my stride. I was no longer struggling to maintain my grades—I was now thriving, working as hard as I could. When representatives from The Shopping Center Network in

Miami came to Bauder, I sat in my marketing classroom tapping my pen on the desk with excitement. The recruiters were asking for applicants for their new program—*The Beautiful You Tour*. They were looking for young people to represent large corporations, including Maybelline and Clairol. The group would travel around the country on tour. Together, the team would go from city to city setting up shows and offering free makeovers to showcase the brands. I couldn't wait to get home and fill out the application.

In the days that followed submitting my application, I spent every free waking moment using my imagination to call in exactly what I wanted. In the same way I'd rested on my bed and dreamed of Costa Rica, I began to construct my vision of being on *The Beautiful You Tour*. I imagined myself waking up in a hotel, slipping on a new dress and shoes before heading out the door to meet other members of the tour. I pictured the way the hallways in the hotel would smell—like fresh linens and expensive perfume. I'd imagine myself heading to the local mall with colleagues, preparing for the show, then ending the day dancing the night away in the trendiest nightclubs. I could feel the experience with all of my senses.

Although I was able to maintain the vision most of the time, of course, there were moments of doubt. I noticed that I was fighting an internal battle to remind myself that *I was worthy*. After all, I'd had a lifetime of evidence that I wasn't good enough. It took discipline and practice to break the cycle of the thoughts and beliefs that were so engrained. I knew I had to keep at it. We become, after all, what we believe about ourselves.

My hands shook as I read the letter again, and again, and again. I could hardly believe the words even though they were staring me in the face in black and white. Hired. I was hired! They'd offered me the job with a good salary and a weekly per diem. In two weeks, I'd fly to Phoenix to meet up with the rest of the tour and get ready to learn the ropes. I hadn't been on a plane since the trip to Costa Rica. Now, I would board a plane to my future.

For the next eighteen months, I traveled the country learning more than I had in my two years of college. On nights out, I was partying with the rich and famous. I met *Wonder Woman*, Linda Carter, the spokesmodel at the time for Maybelline. On our stop in Chicago, I danced all night in the famous Limelight VIP room with UB40. I stayed at the Plaza Hotel in Manhattan and danced at the Fun House on the Lower West Side to DJ Jellybean Benitez alongside his famous fiancé at the time ... Madonna.

I was beginning to live the life I had always dreamed of.

Sometimes at night, I would think back to the moments in my childhood when things were at their worst. As I tossed and turned, I thought about young me. I saw her petrified with the cold barrel of a gun pressed to her head. I saw her lost and alone being shamed for wetting the bed. I wondered what she'd think about the version of me she'd see today. I'd close my eyes and imagine her happy face. Her beautiful, brown eyes bright, her smile big and wide, proud of who she'd become.

Since the only constant in life is change, as time wore on, I began to feel tired of the big energy of the tour. Having spent much of my childhood alone, my soul needed quiet time. My favorite thing to do in a new city was to wander the streets, heading into shops and exploring hidden corners. On days off, I loved to find small, independent local bookstores.

During a trip to San Francisco, I woke up one Monday morning ready to explore. I'd heard about an old book shop in the financial district, so I decided to make the trek. I headed out into the fog, up and down hilly streets, wandering for what seemed like hours. Finally, I turned the corner and saw it—one of the most quaint, old bookshops I'd ever set eyes on. I walked up to the door and opened it; a small bell rang as the door swung open and shut. The inside of the store smelled like old paper and dust. It was delicious. I ran my hands along the spines of books, letting myself feel the magnitude of the space—how many authors' enlightened thoughts were expressed in those books. I loved the feeling of being among such greatness.

As I made my way through the shop, the wood floor creaking beneath my feet, I stopped suddenly noticing a small book on the floor right in front of me. I bent down and picked it up—*You* by Frances Wilshire, published in 1935. Breathless, I thought, *this is a sign*. I brought the book to the counter and paid for it.

I tucked the book under my arm and headed to a local café. There, sipping a latte, I read the book cover-to-cover. It was as if every word spoke to my soul. The book said what I heard Spirit say to me so many years ago. *I am a Divine child, and my birthright is to be happy*. Chapters were entitled, "The Law of Attraction", "The Law of Equilibrium", and more. My favorite part of the book read:

"You must first give your entire attention to the improvement of yourself. You must spend time, effort and money on yourself. You must first have strength, vitality, wisdom or money to be able to give and thereby to fulfill the second half, which in other words, is service. You cannot take out of a bag what is not in it. You cannot give unless you have something to give."[10]

Although the book was written in the 1930s, it was as if it was written for me. I felt as though my soul remembered the teachings.

I devoured the book not once but so many times that I could quote it from memory. I began to change the way I looked at myself and the world, devouring books on manifestation, transformation, alchemy, and other metaphysical concepts. I opened my mind and heart to thinking and believing differently and yet, it felt like I was finally naming and solidifying beliefs I'd long held. It felt like a homecoming—familiar. It felt like Truth.

By the time I was finished with the tour, I had saved thousands in per diem. I returned home to Mom's in Ft Lauderdale, bought a used Volkswagen Jetta and decided not to return the next year. I was tired of living out of a suitcase.

I loved watching *The Oprah Winfrey Show* and caught as many of her interviews as I could. I was inspired by many of the guests, especially

10 Frances Wilshire, *You* (Willing Publishing Company, 1935)

those who focused on spirituality, psychology, and personal growth. One day, as I sat on my couch, journal in hand, I watched an episode featuring Dr. Brian Weiss. He was discussing his book about reincarnation called *Many Lives, Many Masters*. After the show was over, I immediately headed to the library to check out a copy.

I spent that evening snuggled into bed reading the book cover to cover. It opened my mind up to a thought I had never pondered before; *what if my soul chose my parents?* This simple reframe began to empower me. I wasn't a victim of my childhood; I was a powerful, wise soul to have chosen these experiences. When I thought about it this way, I noticed my body was flooded by a feeling of strength. As I tuned in to Spirit, I felt I was getting a clear sign that this was Truth for me.

*Chapter 24*

# MY GREATEST TEACHER

〜 *1988* 〜

*Speak to us of Children.*
*And he said:*
*Your children are not your children.*
*They are the sons and daughters of Life's longing for itself.*
*They come through you but not from you,*
*And though they are with you yet they belong not to you.*
*You may give them your love but not your thoughts,*
*For they have their own thoughts.*
*You may house their bodies but not their souls,*
*For their soul's dwell in the house of tomorrow, which you cannot visit,*
*not even in your dreams.*
*You may strive to be like them but seek not to make them like you.*
*For life goes not backward nor tarries with yesterday.*
*You are the bows from which your children as living*
*arrows are sent forth.*
*The archer sees the mark upon the path of the infinite, and He bends*
*you with His might that His arrows may go swift and far.*
*Let your bending in the archer's hand be for gladness;*

JANA WILSON

*For even as He loves the arrow that flies, so He loves*
*also the bow that is stable.* [11]
—Khalil Gibran The Prophet

Finally, home from tour, I was ready to be responsible. I got a job selling Hyundai's and met a man named Curt who was 35, thirteen years older than me. He was the finance manager at the dealership. Curt came from a well-to-do family and appeared to be stable—certainly more stable than anyone I had previously dated. Things started off quickly and within the first week, we were sleeping together.

At 22, I had learned the signs of pregnancy in my body. The very first time I had sex with Curt, within minutes, I knew I was pregnant.

"How can you possibly know that?" he asked, turning on his side to face me.

"I've been pregnant before—I know my body."

That night, in the light of the moon streaming through the open window, I did something I'd never done before. I cradled my belly.

Previously, when I got pregnant, I immediately made an appointment with a clinic to terminate. This time, however, was completely different. I'd been doing so much work on myself. I'd been learning about our souls and how they are connected. I was tied to the spirit in my womb, I knew this baby was there for a reason—this was *my* baby. She wasn't just with me now. It felt like she had been with me for eons before, living life alongside me. Her presence was calming, soothing, comforting. I knew one thing to be true—this soul was tethered to mine and she was *my purpose*.

I expected Curt to put up a fight and ask me to terminate, but to my surprise, he was thrilled when I told him that I had decided to move forward with the pregnancy. He rented a beachfront condo for us to live in while I moved through the pregnancy. There, to the chorus of crashing waves, and long lazy afternoons reading and napping, I'd spend my time

---

11 Khalil Gibran, "On Children" (1923)

connecting with the life taking shape inside me.

As my belly swelled, I loved spending time on the beach, walking every morning and evening, enjoying the foamy water lapping at my toes. After my walks, I'd sit on the balcony with a book, devouring slices of cold watermelon with salt, and listening to the waves roar and crash against the shore as I turned pages. With each inhale and exhale I found myself grateful for everything. This life I had inside me felt holy. I would do for my unborn child what I hadn't been able to do for myself—create stability.

One sunny morning, I woke with a tightness in my belly that I hadn't yet felt. So close to my due date, I knew there was a possibility I could be experiencing the early stages of labor. I went about my day, taking my morning walk and making lunch. The sensations were ebbing and flowing, changing shape. Those first feelings of tightness were now accompanied by piercing pain. I'd taken Lamaze classes and had prepared myself for a natural birth, so I did my best to breathe through each contraction and push the fear away.

I was able to labor alone for a time, but eventually called Curt to come home. It was time to head to the hospital.

After he evaluated me, my obstetrician, Dr. Scheinberg, informed me that I wasn't in active labor. He said that I was having Braxton-Hick's contractions, which meant the baby wasn't ready to come yet. Seeing my anxiety, Dr. Scheinberg sat down next to me and took my hand in his. He looked deeply into my eyes and said in the gentlest way, "Jana, I want you to go home, find a mirror, and talk to your inner child. I want you to tell her that she will still have fun when the baby comes. Tell her life is going to be amazing."

I looked back at him with tears in my eyes and nodded in agreement. It was as if he could read my mind, intuiting just how nervous I was about having a baby, unmarried at twenty-two.

When I left the hospital, I did exactly as Dr. Scheinberg prescribed, I went directly home and walked into the bathroom, locking the door behind me. I sat on the floor in front of the mirror, my belly resting in my lap. I gazed into my dark brown eyes, drew a breath and willed the words to come. Yet, nothing came, only tears. I quickly averted my eyes, staring down at the tile floor. I had never looked into a mirror and stared into my own eyes. I had looked at myself, but not *into* myself. The intimacy—it was all too much. I let the tears roll down my cheeks as I opened my eyes and forced myself to look again. As I peered into my eyes, all I could see was a frightened child—Little Jana cowering within. Through quiet sobs, I began to speak softly, "Jana, I'm here for you, I will always be here for you."

My heart softened.

My body relaxed.

The baby moved.

The baby wiggled from deep in my womb, stretching out and deforming my belly. It was as if she was signaling that she could feel me, acknowledging the connection that I'd finally allowed myself to make.

A few days later, I finally surrendered the resistance. After twenty-two hours of natural labor, I delivered my angel and greatest teacher, Taylor Rae. She was 8 pounds 1.5 oz and perfect in every way.

"Hi Precious Angel. Welcome to the world."

Curt placed his arms around me and smiled. "She's perfect."

That evening, in the low light of the hospital room, I held Taylor in my arms. I stared deep into her eyes, experiencing a connection unlike anything I had ever felt before. This tiny human being, this immense soul, was so familiar that it felt like a reunion rather than something new. There, in the space where the veil between Heaven and Earth is so very thin, I felt whole in a way I never had before.

Early motherhood was beautiful. Still in the beach condo, I was living in a balance of breastfeeding, diaper changes, and soft coos from my sweet baby. There was something so magical about that time, getting to ease into motherhood in such a tranquil place. The sweet, salty air swirled through the house as seagulls offered shrill squeals as they swooped through the sky. Together, Taylor and I walked the beach, her warm little body swaddled against mine as I strolled, holding her close.

As dreamy as this period of time was, the lease was up on the condo, and we had to return to Curt's parents' winter residence in Plantation, 45 minutes inland. It was a hard transition for me; moving into a house owned by his family. It wasn't something I ever wanted. When I met Curt, he led me to believe that the Plantation house was *his* home. However, like most things I was learning with Curt, it was a trick of the light. He was comfortable living a life of half-truths and blatant lies.

I was beginning to sense that things with Curt may be reaching a fever pitch, his behaviors were becoming unpredictable. He would fawn over Taylor and me when he was home, often bringing me flowers and taking us out to fancy restaurants. He'd sing softly to Taylor while putting her down for a nap and bounce her when she was fussy. However, this only lasted so long. He'd also stay out late, coming home slurring his words and making excuses for where he'd been. History had told me it would only be a matter of time before things hit a wall. And I was right.

*Crash!*

I sat straight up and put my hand on the edge of Taylor's bassinet. The digital clock read 3:03 am. The sound had come from downstairs. I felt the bed next to me and Curt wasn't there. My heart was pounding. I guessed he was in the kitchen making himself a snack after his late night out with friends.

I rubbed my eyes and quietly got out of bed, making my way to the stairs. I tip-toed down each one, careful not to make too much noise. When I landed at the bottom of the stairs, I turned to face the kitchen entrance and caught sight of Curt. He was standing over the stove holding a spoon with white powder and liquid on it, heating it with the flame.

I quickly turned and tip-toed back up the stairs, got into bed, and pulled the covers tight to my chin. My chest was tight. My breath was short. My mind was swimming. I had ignored the signs, preoccupied with the baby.

The next day when Curt went to work, I packed up all our things and moved back to my mom's. I felt like a failure. All the false beliefs came rushing back to the surface.

*You aren't good enough. If you were, he would have stopped drinking and using drugs.*

I convinced myself that I was somehow responsible for his addictions. In a flash of wisdom, I clearly saw that I was a caretaker just like my mom. And with Curt, I was in a highly dysfunctional relationship with a *taker*. I was repeating the pattern modeled by my parents—codependency. These behaviors pointed to one difficult truth: I was still unconsciously trying to save my daddy.

Back at Mom's house, I lifted Taylor out of her crib, swaddled her in a blanket, looked into her eyes and promised, "for you, I'll be better."

I held her in my arms and let my mind wander, allowing my heart to open to the answers I'd been seeking. I thought about Mack, Curt, and all the men in between. I began to come to an awareness that there was a common denominator in all the relationships I had attracted—*me*. I needed to look within. With this newfound awareness came a giddy feeling of anticipation. If I could figure out how to unlearn the conditioning from my childhood, then I could attract and create a healthy relationship with a man, giving me and Taylor the life we deserved. I watched as she slept, her pursed lips moving softly. I knew I could do it; I was a 'can-do girl' just like Mom said.

In the coming weeks, I began to attend Alcoholics Anonymous, Al-Anon, Narcotic Anonymous, and Adult Children of Alcoholic meetings. When it was my turn to share, I'd begin with, "Hi, I'm Jana and I'm an adult child of an alcoholic." I'd then allow my intuition to guide what story I shared.

At each meeting, I listened intently, allowing their stories to fill me up. Humans are storytellers and sharing our stories is how we connect. Of course, this is cathartic for a time, but that catharsis can only take us so far. We must be willing to give up the story we've lived, so that we can create the new story we want to live. I was ready to break free from the chains of my old narrative and part ways with the toxic dynamic I'd learned from my family of origin.

*Chapter 25*

# CONFRONTING THE PAST
## 1989

I leaned closer to the mirror, my lips parted as I swiped mascara on my lashes. I then leaned back and surveyed my face, deciding I needed a little more blush, and maybe a red lip. I glanced over at Taylor while she played quietly in her playpen, giggling softly as she stacked cups. I ruffled her hair before rummaging through my closet. I was headed out to a club with some new friends I made at the restaurant where I had been working part-time for several months.

As I pulled a skirt and top from my closet, I heard Mom's heavy foot-steps. Then, the door to my room flew open. "Jana!" she yelled. "Get the hell out here!" She left the door open as she stomped back to the kitchen.

I drew a breath. My stomach dropped. This was something I'd come to expect from Mom. Now a mom myself, I was finding it difficult to live with her. There were fewer nights sitting in the lamplight reading. Less time talking about feelings and digging into astrology and other spiritual topics she'd come to love. Instead, there was bickering, and big, angry outbursts over seemingly insignificant things. I was now back in school, taking all psychology classes. I began to look at my feelings more closely and pay attention to the way our relationship stayed the same, despite my own personal growth. With every hug, kiss, and moment of loving connection with Taylor, my childhood trauma was beginning to surface. My heart could hardly hold the love I had for my daughter. And I knew that I would never, ever make the choices for Taylor that Mom had made for Roy and me.

I headed out of my room and toward the kitchen where Mom was clattering dishes around in the sink. As I walked into the doorway, Mom yelled, "You were supposed to clean this kitchen! What are you doing getting ready to go out? You think you're leaving here with this kitchen in shambles?!"

"No, Mom I just hadn't had time yet to—"

"YOU'RE FILLED WITH EXCUSES!" She grabbed a wet, soapy dish from the sink and brought it down as hard as she could on the floor – then another, and another. Each dish getting closer and closer to my feet as they shattered, sending shards of porcelain spraying in my direction. Blood streaked my legs as the slivers of dishes ripped shallow cuts in my skin. Although I was scared, the sound of my heartbeat booming in my ears, I steadied myself focusing on breathing slow and deep. I let Mom continue her rant until she was tired—I knew she couldn't regulate her emotions; I had to let her rage until she was done. I was beginning to practice my ability to witness emotional triggers and not react.

Finally, she took the last dish from the sink and stood there staring at me, breathless. "You're going to clean this up."

I stood still, blood trickling down my legs, and stared back at her. Out of breath, she reached for her pack of Virginia Slims and lit one. When I was a child living in constant chaos, these outbursts were common. Now, as I stood calm and quiet in the stillness of our shared home, her outburst seemed out of place—alien. I knew it was time that I face my fears and speak to Mom about her behavior. Not just her behavior now, but how she'd behaved for my entire life. I needed to approach her mom-to-mom.

The next day, once the pile of broken dishes that carpeted the kitchen was cleaned up, I put Taylor down for her nap and asked Mom if she would come sit down with me. I sat calmly on the couch as she joined me.

"Mom, we need to talk about yesterday," I began.

"What about yesterday?" she asked, glaring at me.

"About what happened in the kitchen. What triggered you to lose your temper like that?"

"You know full well what triggered me. You do nothing in this house and just expect me to clean up after you. I've had enough."

"I hear you," I responded. "But that doesn't mean you should fly off the handle like that. That behavior scares me, and Taylor was just in the next room."

"Oh, don't give me that crap like I'm a *bad grandmother*. You don't pay rent here."

"Right, but Granny bought this house for you, and you don't pay her rent. Isn't that what parents do for their kids? Help them so they don't have to struggle?"

"Well, if you contributed more, maybe I wouldn't get so angry at you. Did you ever think of that?"

I closed my eyes. I knew it was time—I needed to have the conversation with her that I had avoided for nearly fifteen years. "Mom, this has always been a problem with you. Let's not forget the shotgun. Roy and me? You threatened to kill us. You held a gun to our heads! How can you possibly think that I'm the problem? You've always been like this—so completely volatile."

She looked at me with her eyebrows knitted together. "Oh, come on. That never happened." She shook her head.

"Are you kidding?" I asked, incredulous.

"Are *you* kidding? That never happened. What a sick thing to say," she spat.

"Yes, it did. When I was nine, before you went away to the hospital. We'd just come back from being with Dad and you were angry and wanted to know everything about our time with him. We didn't have anything to tell you, and you picked up a shotgun and held it to our heads. You told us that you'd kill us right there."

"I did no such thing. How dare you," she replied, lighting a cigarette, visibly agitated, glaring at me through eyes of disdain.

"You don't believe me? Fine." I picked up the phone from its base. "I'm calling Roy."

I placed the phone on speaker. When Roy picked up, I explained what had happened and what I'd just told Mom about the gun incident. "Mom doesn't believe it happened. Can you tell her?"

Mom stared at the phone in disbelief as Roy recalled in vivid color the events of that night, how terrified we were, how her friend wrestled the gun from her, and how Aunt Ginny came to get us. Tears rolled down her face as I hung up the phone and put my arm around her. She looked up at me, her eyes brimming with tears. She looked like a wounded child.

"I knew something horrible had happened to land me in the hospital, but I had no idea what it was. I only remembered shadows of that night— bits and pieces."

"I'm sorry, Mom. I had no idea you didn't remember it."

"I was so torn up about your father. I was on a heavy dose of Valium and was drinking that day. I blacked out. I don't remember anything about that night. I knew by the way everyone reacted that it was awful, but no matter how much work I did in the hospital, I could never pull up the memory. I never wanted to ask anyone about it either. I just did my best to move forward."

She began to weep, her shoulders softly moving up and down with each sob. I opened my arms. She collapsed into me, letting me hold her and stroke her hair until she was spent. She looked me in the eyes and began talking—she opened up about the details of her childhood, about losing her dad so young, and all the ways in which she felt responsible for his death. She shared with me how Granny wasn't there for her, which led her to try to kill herself—wanting the pain of losing her daddy to go away.

"I know I made a lot of mistakes with you and Roy. I do, I know that. I really tried though." She sniffed. "I tried."

She shared about her mental illness and her endless struggle to be happy and content. I held her hands as she continued, sharing things that I didn't know about our life as a family, even filling in all the blanks about Vegas and Atlanta.

We cried together a lot that day and laughed some too. I reminded her how we'd sing along to the song "Let 'Em In" by Wings whenever it came on the radio...

*Someone's knockin' at the door*
*Somebody's ringin' the bell*
*Do me a favor, open the door*

"IT'S ARCHIE," we would add in unison, "DON'T LET HIM IN!"

I held her close, feeling connected. I rubbed Mom's back while I let her stories sink in. I felt nothing but deep gratitude for Mom and her vulnerability. It helped me take the first steps toward something I'd wanted forever—a deeper understanding of my family. And, in effect, a better understanding of myself.

Everyone is operating from their own level of consciousness. We all have a different reality based on how we perceive ourselves and the world. Forgiveness comes naturally when we can see the others perspective. Native Americans have a saying, "walk a mile in his moccasins before you judge." When we are in inquiry vs. accusation, we can open our heart and see the others perspective. It doesn't mean we condone it, what it means is we accept that everyone is at their own level of consciousness, and we don't personalize it. What are you taking personal that someone else has done, that is creating suffering?

*Chapter 26*

# CYCLE BREAKER
## ∽ *1990* ∾

*"If you look deeply into the palm of your hand, you will see your
parents and all generations of your ancestors. All of them are
alive in this moment. Each is present in your body. You are
the continuation of each of these people."* [12]

— Thich Nhat Hanh

ollowing the conversation with Mom, I found my curiosity piqued.
I was hungry to learn about the cycle my family had been stuck
in, since before I was born. I began to devour books on relationships and family dynamics and was beginning to learn about generational trauma. With each book I read, things became clearer. My mom had
opened my eyes to the fact that our family seemed destined for the chaos
we inevitably found ourselves lost in. As I expanded my knowledge and
understanding, Dr. John Bradshaw released a PBS special which helped
me better understand dysfunctional families and the shame that binds

---

12  Thich Nhat Hanh, *Reconciliation: Healing The Inner Child* (Parallax Press, 2006)

them to continue to perpetuate the dysfunction. With each book, lecture, and lesson I devoured, I was able to unpack more of my past. I was the *family disrupter* the one who would say what everyone else was thinking but lacked the courage to say. It became crystal clear to me that I was the healthiest person in my toxic family. The more I found my voice, the more they tried to silence me.

I thought about Taylor and what our lives would look like as she grew. She and I were our own little family now, and I wanted her to experience peace and joy. I found myself swatting images from my mind, pushing away memories of myself as a child, hiding from Mom and Dad's knock-down drag-out fights, going to bed hungry and feeling less than. I wanted Taylor to feel safe, valued and adored.

Looking at my family's past through a new lens, I recognized the generational trauma that precipitated the madness. It wasn't just Roy and me who were raised in tumultuous circumstances, forced to seek refuge from the turmoil. Mom, Dad, and their parents were also brought up in families who were always living in survival mode. Each of them had developed their own unhealthy responses to the pain they had experienced, I simply refused to let that happen to us. Taylor was my precious angel, and I was committed to breaking the cycle to give her everything she deserved—everything my family deserved, but never claimed.

I set out to become the *cycle-breaker* in my family, and I knew I wouldn't be able to break it on my own. I searched for all resources that could help me take the knowledge I was gathering and put it into action. I began to examine the church I was attending, a non-denominational Christian church. I had started attending services again, wanting Taylor to have the foundation of Jesus' teachings and fall in love with the Holy Spirit. Yet, after the Sunday services I rarely felt inspired or uplifted. I felt judged. The minister spent a lot of time focusing on anti-abortion rallies and doctrine and dogma that felt stifling. I reflected on my experience when I was twelve, when I challenged the Sunday school teacher. Now I was examining my beliefs and it became obvious the church of my childhood was no longer in alignment for me.

A close friend from my days on *The Beautiful You Tour*, had given me *Daily Word*, a devotional book from the Unity Foundation. I researched and found they had churches around the country. I found one nearby in Delray Beach. Unity was a place with a more expansive take on spirituality, taking a practical approach to Christianity. The services were held in a mid-century building with towering windows overlooking a huge, bright, orange Royal Poinciana tree. I learned about false beliefs, meditation, and all other spiritual traditions that parallel and even compliment the teachings of Christianity. I was breaking down the walls of my Pentecostal/Baptist upbringing and was expanding my mind. I felt at home.

Yet, every journey comes with challenges. Roy judged my changing beliefs, warning me about my choice to "stray from Jesus." I wished he could understand. I wasn't straying from Jesus. With the spiritual education I was gaining at Unity, I was learning *practical* Christianity, which was further integrating Jesus' teachings into my life. Unity taught me that God is not a physical man in the sky. Rather, what we call God is energy, and that energy is present in all of creation, everywhere and always. Unity taught me to explore many spiritual lineages and paths. Ultimately, that would lead me to a richer, more intimate understanding of the Divine. I began to look at the criticism I received from family members as a sign that I was on the right path.

As I shifted into this new mindset, I found myself longing to strengthen my spirituality in new ways. I had always prayed and had mystical experiences in childhood, the most profound taking place when I was twelve. Now, however, I was finding practices that allowed me to develop an even closer connection to Spirit.

Each morning, I would wake before sunrise and tiptoe out of my bedroom into the quiet dark living room. While Mom and Taylor still slept, I would sit on the couch in stillness, allowing the silence to drape over me. This simple practice began to ground me in the true nature of reality. I always knew that God was present everywhere, but now I *knew* that God lived, moved and breathed through me. I came to know this as a Divine Spark that exists within each person and all of Creation; this spark seeks to be expressed. These teachings were in alignment with what I felt Spirit had communicated to me as I was cradled so long ago and reminded—*this is not your home*. I was beginning to understand how our thoughts, beliefs and feelings, draw experiences to us. I was learning that everything in the physical realm has its beginning in thought, and I was beginning to dig deeper into my thoughts than ever before.

At Unity, there was a couple who were Deacons in the church and licensed family therapists. They offered counseling sessions on a sliding scale. When I discovered this offering, I booked my appointment with the woman, Julie, right away. In my very first session, I opened up to Julie and shared about my life, telling her things that I had never said out loud to another person. She was loving and accepting, holding space for me to share. Over the next eighteen months, I took a huge leap in healing many of the labels I had been imprisoned by…

*White trash*
*Slut*
*Rape Victim*
*Poor*
*Stupid*
*Single mom*

Working with Julie was another monumental step to excavating and accepting my past.

During this time, I had been waiting tables at a restaurant for the better part of a year while working toward my psychology degree. I didn't mind the job, but I also didn't love it. I was still passionate about fashion and design and longed for a job that would allow me to harness that passion. I began to get extremely clear about my vision for my future, imagining myself working at Bloomingdales in Boca Raton. I pictured myself dressing in the morning, staring in the mirror brushing the apples of my cheeks with blush. I envisioned my ride to the store, entering through an employee entrance, and taking my place amongst beautiful clothes, bespoke accessories, and irresistible makeup; spending my days helping customers purchase items that made them look and feel their best. Of course, negative thoughts and fears tried to work their way in. They whispered *I'm not good enough* in the back of my mind, urging me to drop the fantasy and settle for what was in front of me. In the past, I might have given into these fears, letting the voice in my head become louder and louder until it shut me down. Now, however, I was learning to silence the critical voice, focus on what I wanted and make headway toward my next dream.

One sunny afternoon before my shift at the restaurant, I made my way to Bloomingdales. As the door slid open, my heart felt full. The smell of perfume filled my nostrils as I made my way to the counter to ask for an application, which I filled out on the spot. The next day, I received a call from a manager. I was invited for an interview.

Recognizing that the manifestation was working, I spent the next few days preparing for the interview by exploring every angle of my imagination. Each morning before sunrise, I sat and traced every inch of the store in my imagination. I performed the duties. I let myself feel the rush of excitement that would come with each shift.

On the day of my interview, however, I woke with anxiety. As I dressed in my carefully chosen outfit and did my makeup to perfection, nagging doubts began to surface.

*I'm not good enough.*

These thoughts led to an overall feeling of insecurity, which manifested in physical feelings of panic. As I drove to the store, towering palm trees casting pulsing shadows on my car, I reminded myself of something I'd recently learned; a mantra rooted in manifestation. *Fake it until you make it.*

I walked through the parking lot and headed into the store, a rush of cool air hitting my face as the door slid open. I strolled inside, my heels clicking on the tile floor as I repeated *fake it until you make it* over and over in my mind.

I greeted the hiring manager with a firm handshake and answered every question with precision and confidence. The more confident I sounded, the more confident I felt. Each time the interviewer nodded at one of my answers, my heart soared. The manifestation had worked—I was hired on the spot, given a position as a counter manager for Germaine Monteil. I put in my notice at the restaurant and started at Bloomingdales as soon as I could.

On my first day, I drove to the store in my red convertible VW Cabriolet, which Curt was still paying for. That morning, I strutted into the store and took my place behind the counter and learned the ropes from a woman named Lisa. She was warm and chatty and immediately welcomed me, introducing me to the other ladies in the department.

Those first few weeks were a beautiful blur. Lisa took me under her wing and, since she was respected and loved by all the other girls in the department, I was instantly part of the gang, forging bonds that we'd have for life. On days off, we began going to the beach together, lazing in the sun or playing games of volleyball, the waves crashing at our feet.

After one afternoon at the beach, one of the girls dropped me off at home. As I walked up to the door, I noticed that my car wasn't there. I opened the door to the house and called, "Mom! Where's my car?"

Mom appeared in the hallway holding Taylor, looking at me with sad eyes. "I'm so sorry Honey, some men came and towed it away."

"Why?" I cried out.

"They said Curt was behind on payments. It was repossessed," she said, patting Taylor's back.

I felt deflated. Hot tears pricked the backs of my eyes. Without Curt's financial help, I would need to find a way to stand on my own, but it wouldn't be easy. I only had about $500 left in my savings account, and my salary at Bloomingdales was just $250 a week. I couldn't wait to save, and I didn't have any credit. I needed a car *now*. I'd have to get creative.

I went out and began searching for a solution as soon as I could. That's when I found it at a small dealership that mostly sold junk cars—a 'hooptie'. In contrast to the cute, glossy convertible, the enormous, red Oldsmobile was rusty around the edges. It had no AC and only had AM radio, but it would get me around town, regardless of how humiliated I felt driving it. I couldn't bring myself to park it at the Town Center in Boca, so I parked as far away as possible and walked to the store each day. By the time I arrived at work my fine hair would be limp and stuck to my head from the sweltering heat and humidity. I hated the feeling of stepping behind the counter coated in sweat, dabbing at my runny makeup before facing customers.

Even a 'hooptie', however, can have a silver lining. On my way to work every day, without the luxury of FM radio, I was left to explore what was available on AM stations. That's when I discovered a radio station that would add new layers to my self-exploration—a personal development station with motivational content. I would listen to speakers like Tony Robbins, Susan Jeffers and Les Brown talking about mindset and beliefs and how we create our reality through our thoughts. I was spending every commute solidifying my new empowering beliefs, disciplining myself to think differently.

The more I listened, the more encouraged I felt to continue my manifestation practices. As I drove to work each day, I began my visualization exercises. With the windows down, my hair blowing wildly in the wind, I would envision myself driving a small Honda civic. I pictured the sporty car with an automatic transmission, AC and an AM/FM radio complete with a cassette player. As I commuted from Mom's house in Pompano Beach to the ritzy town of Boca, I would picture myself with gratitude driving in my new car. I would smile wide, even let out a laugh at times, acting out how I would feel driving my Honda.

One day at work, I stood behind the counter arranging products between consultations with customers. That's when a debonair man in his late 50's walked up to me, smiling wide.

"Hi," I chirped. "How can I help you?"

"Are you Jana?" he asked.

"I am," I smiled, wondering how he knew my name.

He stuck out his hand. "I'm William Walle III, but you can call me Bill."

I took his hand. "Nice to meet you, Bill. Can I help you with something?"

"You and I have a mutual acquaintance" he said with a big smile.

"Really, who is that?"

"Cheryl Mumford." Cheryl had been a close friend for several years, but I had outgrown the friendship. We weren't on a similar path—she was interested in the party scene and disinterested in personal development and spirituality.

"She shared with me about your life as a single mom," he said, his eyes sympathetic, with a disarming kindness.

"Oh, wow," I responded, meeting his gaze. "Yes, I'm a single mom. Of course, there are challenges, but I just love my daughter so much. It's all worth it."

"Can I take you to lunch at the food court today?"

I hesitated for a moment, hoping he wouldn't think it was a date, but I pushed the thought aside. "Sure," I said.

That day at lunch, Bill was kind and caring, asking me questions about Taylor and my life in general. There was no hint that he expected anything romantic, he was simply a nice man expressing interest in my life.

Over the next few months, Bill would stop by periodically and take me to lunch. Conversation always centered around Taylor, my life, and my spiritual journey, which was continuing to develop. Bill was on a similar journey of self-inquiry and, together, we'd discuss philosophy and religion, each sharing how our relationship with Spirit was deepening. Bill was attending a weekly class on *A Course in Miracles* and invited me to come with him. He even bought me my book for the class. The teachings of the

CIM changed my life, broadening my understanding of miracles and our role in making miracles happen. It is in this class where I discovered the teachings of Marianne Williamson—an author who had been on Oprah talking about her book, *Return to Love*. The teachings on love and its role in achieving inner peace were mind-altering. I was able to look at myself differently, not only as someone with the ability to manifest, but someone with the ability to make miracles. That knowledge unlocked even more confidence in my personal power.

That year on my birthday, Bill gave me a card. I opened it as he watched, a sly smile spread across his face. As I pulled it from the envelope, a check fell out. When I saw the amount, I lost my breath—$2,500. I reached out and wrapped him in a tight hug. Granny was the only one who had ever done anything so generous for me.

"Thank you, thank you," I said, squeezing him as tightly as I could.

He pulled back and looked me in the eye. "Jana, I just want to help you get a safe, reliable car for you and Taylor. You both deserve this and more." Bill was an angel in our life.

That day, I left work in my hooptie and drove straight to a reputable dealership. There, I found a 5-year-old automatic Honda Civic with air conditioning, AM/FM radio, and a cassette player! In that moment, I thought back to my rides to and from work, smiling, feeling gratitude for things that were to come. A tingling sensation came over me as I realized I could manifest positive things in my life by focusing my attention on feelings of gratitude. In thanking the Universe for blessings yet to come, I was preparing myself to receive and setting intentions that were being magnified by positive thought. I was learning that the more I believed and the more gratitude I put out there, the more I was given. As I stepped into my new Civic to drive it to work for the first time, I was filled with an overwhelming sense of satisfaction. I reached forward and turned on the radio, still choosing to listen to the AM station I had come to love. I was hungry for more knowledge, craving for a deeper understanding of the power I was wielding. I was coming to learn that as I harnessed my own power, the Universe had my back. All my self-doubt and fear were beginning to morph into something new: *acceptance of my own power*.

## Chapter 27

# EVICTION
### ⤳ *1995* ⤲

*"Life is always happening for us, not to us."*[13]
—Tony Robbins

O ver the next couple of years, I enjoyed the steady rhythm of my work at Bloomingdales. I was still in the routine of waking up each morning to meditate before getting Taylor ready for daycare and heading to work. During my commute, I continued to listen to educational, inspirational content. I was learning so much more about myself and the magic that existed within me. At night, I'd slide a cassette of positive affirmations into my Walkman, and drift into deep slumber reprogramming my mind to think and believe differently. I was consistent in devoting my time to rewiring my mind. I was adopting new beliefs like "I am valuable, I am good, and I am loveable." I was diligently practicing thinking differently. My new thoughts were solidifying into new empowering beliefs.

---

13 Tony Robbins, *Tony Robbins: I Am Not Your Guru* (Netflix, 2016)

Although I liked my job in retail, some things about the job were less than ideal. The hours were all over the place and often included weekends, which was tough on me as a single mother. Taylor was growing—becoming a sweet, talkative little girl with a compassionate heart. She would gather her stuffed animals and put them in a pile, and say, "Mommy let's give these to the poor children." I was implementing what I was learning about conscious parenting from Unity and all of the books I was consuming. When Taylor made bad choices, I would say, "You're a good girl, you just made a bad choice." Separating her actions from who she was.

I hated missing any moment I could spend with her; she was my everything. I started envisioning myself with a job that would allow me to spend more time with her, mapping out in my mind what an ideal day would look like, and expressing gratitude as if it were already mine.

One day, an older woman named Carol, came into the store, and approached the makeup counter needing advice on products she could use to elevate her look. I looked at her skin tone and gathered foundation, blush, eye shadow, and brushes. I wiped her face clean and began dabbing foundation on with a makeup sponge. "Your skin is already glowing!" I said.

"I've needed to do this for so long. I figured my lunch break would be a good time!" she responded with a smile.

"Oh, I agree. What else are lunch breaks for?" I laughed. "So, where do you work?"

"I'm the President of the local Merrill Lynch branch," she replied. "And you? Obviously, I know you work here, but what else? Do you have children?"

I brushed blush on her cheeks and dabbed neutral eyeshadow on her lids while telling her about Taylor and life with Mom. She asked me questions about my aspirations, my dreams and desires. I answered each question honestly and with a soft smile.

"Okay, we're all done. You look stunning," I said, handing her a mirror.

Her eyes widened as she brought the mirror to her face. "Oh, wow.

Jana, you did an excellent job. I'll take every product you used!"

"Wonderful!" I said, walking around the counter to the register.

She placed the mirror on her lap and looked up at me. "Listen, talking to you has been wonderful. I really believe you're going to go so far. In fact, there is an open position at my firm that I think you'd be a perfect fit for. How about you come to my office tomorrow and interview?"

I was taken aback, unsure of what to say so I nodded and blurted out, "Of course, I would love that."

Smiling, she took the bag from my hands, stood from the stool and reached her hand out to shake mine. "I'll see you then." She handed me her business card and left.

The next day, I pulled on dress pants and a jacket and headed to the Merrill Lynch office in Boca Raton. Nervous, I held my purse tightly against my side as I walked toward the door, the stiff chill of the air-conditioning hitting me as the door slid open.

The interview took place in a conference room with a hiring manager in a perfectly pressed suit. She nodded as I answered her questions, making sure to highlight my availability and eagerness. I was elated when I was hired on the spot. I'd finally have a chance to work banker's hours, giving me plenty of time to spend with Taylor so I could provide the stability she deserved. Not only that, but I would also get benefits, and an opportunity to become an investment broker if things went well. I accepted the position immediately, proud that I had used my ability to manifest to make a big, sweeping change.

At first, the job was ideal. I was organized and motivated, always anticipating the needs of the stockbrokers I was assisting. I'd ask questions and get tasks done efficiently and thoughtfully. Carol had become a mentor for me, offering advice and help anytime I needed it. Soon, however, things began to take a sinister turn. The sexual discrimination and harassment I experienced was relentless. Men would grab my ass in the hallway, corner me in the supply closet and try to kiss me and would find ways to whisper in my ear all the sexual things they wanted to do to me. I walked into work with a pit in my stomach every day, trying to convince myself that I could do anything to maintain this stable life for Taylor. However, there was only so much I could endure. I told my Carol about the incidents, and she told me that I needed to dress more demurely, or I would continue to attract this attention. I was baffled. There I was, showing up to work every day in a suit, and I was being told that *I* was the problem. I took a breath and reframed—I needed to set boundaries.

I began to call the men out for treating me this way, and to my surprise, this led to disciplinary action taken against *me*. I was eventually called into Carol's office and put on a corrective action plan due to the many complaints from the brokers that I was argumentative and not following directions. I held firm to my boundaries—I was learning to embrace my *inner bitch*.

Of course, I could only last so long in an environment like that.

After eighteen months, I put in my notice—coincidentally, when the Clarence Thomas hearings based on the accusations of Anita Hill were taking place. I took a risk and left, finding a job as an assistant to a successful female Real Estate broker in Boca. Unfortunately, my new boss, who was generous with me; had late-stage colon cancer and passed away eight months after I began working for her, leaving me with no real prospects.

During this time, Mom left to care for Granny whose health was failing. She'd had a massive heart attack and then required surgery to have a pacemaker placed inside. Not long after the surgery, she fell, and did not last long after that. I curled up in my bed and imagined my sweet granny holding me close. I pictured us at breakfast when she taught me to be 'a lady,' her smell, her laugh, her huge heart. Granny wasn't just a lynchpin of my stability; she was a part of the fabric that made me who I was. As devastated as I was, I felt stable within. The spiritual work I had been doing allowed me to move through her death with grace. She didn't deserve to suffer. As Granny left her body, her soul embarked on a new journey, and I feel her presence with me always. Love is eternal.

Not long after, my granny's burial, we received news that Uncle Buddy had late-stage lung cancer caused by asbestos. Days after burying Granny, Mom decided to quit her job to be by his side.

A few weeks after Mom left, I packed the car for the weekend and headed up north to Suwannee. I wanted to be with my uncle one last time. I gripped the wheel as Taylor played with her doll in the back seat and let my mind wander.

*Hold the fish tight, Jana Lee.*

*Here, scrape it just like this.*

*He's floppin' around like crazy!*

Tall pine trees sped past, giving way to long flat stretches of farmland. We were getting closer. Uncle Buddy had bought land that sat directly on an inlet, at the intersection of the Suwannee River and the Gulf of Mexico. The year before he was diagnosed with lung cancer, he had finished his dream home: a simple fisherman's house set high on stilts. This was the place where he would retire.

Taylor and I arrived before dark, and Mom ushered us into his bedroom. When he saw us, his face lit up, his smile revealing his signature mouthful of bright, white teeth. When people complimented him on his teeth he would always reply, "The best toothpaste is baking soda and peroxide!"

It felt so good to be in his presence.

At just five-years-old, Taylor tucked herself behind me. Seeing him so thin and weak made her nervous. He managed to look over and say, "Hi, T – T is for Tennessee." It's the way Uncle Buddy always greeted Taylor.

Taylor smiled shyly.

Mom took Taylor for a tour of the house, then outside to walk the property and check the crab traps. I pulled a chair next to his bed, reached out, and took his soft, wrinkled hand in mine. We were quiet for what seemed like eternity. He then broke the awkward silence and rasped, "Tell me the story I love to hear—the one about the trip to Jamaica."

I smiled and nodded. "Of course."

In addition to being a commercial fisherman, Uncle Buddy was also a boilermaker, a freemason, and a large crop farmer. When I had returned from the Shopping Center Network tour, he was living in Jamaica growing strawberries.

"Well," I started, "Granny called me one day and asked me to go with her to visit you in Jamaica. We spent two weeks in Mandeville, high up in the mountains in that huge house the corporate farming company had rented for you."

He nodded.

"One day, you took us to a swimming hole the locals called, 'the blue lagoon.' We had been there for less than an hour, when a small man with dreadlocks, shriveled like a raisin, came flying through the air on a thick braided rope, making a flamboyant splash. He swam to the edge of the lagoon and emerged directly in front of me and Granny *naked as a jaybird*. He then grabbed his penis and began to dance around singing in a broken Jamaican accent: *Me cock, me cock, me cock so big*!"

"That's right," he said, his teeth shining as he smiled.

Uncle Buddy let out a raspy laugh that turned it to a coughing fit. I placed my hand on his arm and continued when the coughing subsided.

When I finished recalling the story, his eyes had closed but his bright smile remained.

It was only seven short months before he passed away. Now Mom and I had to deal with a double loss.

After losing two of the most important people in her life, I knew Mom needed a change. She'd started wandering around the house with an absent look on her face. She was grieving—distant and melancholy. Soon she decided to put the house up for sale so she could move to Texas to be near Roy and his family. After all, she had two grandchildren there, who she wanted to spend more time with.

I understood Mom's decision, but it was hard to accept. We had healed so much in our time living together. I knew it was time to let her go, and for me, at age 27, to live on my own again. Now I needed to find a place to rent that I could afford.

With Taylor in tow, I toured as many places as I could. Each one was less desirable than the last. Finally, I answered an ad about a converted garage apartment for $500 a month. Once we moved in, we made the place our own with furniture we took from Mom's house once it sold. I was making ends meet, but just barely. Sometimes I had trouble affording food.

Out of desperation one evening, I called Curt to ask for help. Taylor and I were hungry and didn't have any food in the apartment or money to buy anything. Within a few hours, Curt showed up at the door with a small sack of food—only enough for Taylor. I had been humiliated by having to ask him for help in the first place, and now he was rubbing my face in it. For the first time in many years, I felt broken and scared.

The next day while Taylor was at school, I came home for a break from a secretarial temp job, and found a note taped to the door. I walked up to the door with my eyes squinted. There, in big block letters, was a phrase I didn't expect to see: EVICTION NOTICE.

Dejected, I crumbled on the floor and erupted into tears. Without a lease, there was nothing I could do. I had no idea how I was going to return to work that day. I was scared and stressed in ways I'd never felt before. In the past, I had Mom or Granny to turn to. Now I had to figure this out all on my own. I lay on the floor holding my hands to my face, defeated, afraid, feeling like a massive failure. I felt so victimized, so abandoned, so alone. Then crystal clear I heard a small voice inside say, *this is happening FOR you not TO you.* In a flash of revelation, I knew I didn't want to live in a garage apartment – I had been complaining about the smell of motor oil and how awful it was since moving in. This wasn't the perfect place for me to raise Taylor, in fact, it was a very small notch above *tolerable*.

In that brief flash of awareness, I got what I call a 'hit.' I remembered

Tony Robbins teaching about 'changing your physiological state' – that we must train the body to behave 'as if' we are already wealthy, healthy and happy, if, we are to become that.

I picked myself up off the floor and immediately began running around the apartment, shouting at the top of my lungs "I'm a millionaire!" This was a process I had learned to do whenever heavy, dense emotions were overcoming me. It's called a 'rampage of appreciation'. Quickly, the negative feelings began to fall away, rolling off me like heavy rocks tumbling down a cliff. I became lighter, my heart blossomed open, and the feeling of gratitude filled me. I intuitively picked up my black address book that sat on the counter and opened it to a page that contained the name of someone I had met a few years prior, during my membership classes at Unity. His name was Bruce, he heard my story of being a single mom one evening in class and knew how steadfast I was working to change my life. He was inspired by my motivation to grow and create a better life for my daughter. I closed my eyes and pictured his face. Then I remembered it. He had told me to call him if I ever needed help.

I picked up my beeper and paged him. I immediately got a return beep. I went to a convenience store to call him from a payphone. I stood at the phone playing with the receiver when he answered, "Hello?"

"It's Jana! Gosh, it's so good to talk to you, it's been so long."

"Man, this is so wild. You will not believe it. Just a few moments ago I asked for a sign. I'm looking to replace a member of my staff who quit today, and I need the position filled immediately. Would you be interested?"

"I am—I'm actually working as a temp right now, so I have availability."

"Well, this is a little better than a temp job," he laughed. "I think you'd be perfect for it."

I began to get excited.

"How would you feel about travel?" he asked.

"Great, I can travel!" I responded.

"Fantastic. There are no special skills required. It's a courier position. I need someone to take documents to and from my offshore office. All flights are covered—I have a private jet."

I was intrigued. I asked questions and found out that I would be required to travel to Paradise Island, Bahamas, and Grand Cayman, to retrieve documents. I would be paid very well—$2,000 each trip. I was in shock!

"This is too good to be true," I said, my eyes narrow. "You're not a drug dealer, are you?"

Bruce laughed, "No, no. My family owns a private aircraft company that has offices offshore. The documents we trade are extremely confidential and time sensitive."

The next day, he took me to lunch. As we spoke, I began to share what I had been going through and was honest about my financial situation. "This is a miracle." I confessed.

He smiled wide and nodded. We talked at length about all we had learned through the teachings at Unity. "You know, I've always asked Spirit to be used in ways to help others. This is a blessing for both of us."

Later that day, I reached out to Mom in Texas. I told her about the eviction notice, Curt's awful behavior and how stressful things had been. Then I shared about my new job, giving her every exciting detail.

"I am so happy for you, Honey," she said. I could tell she was beaming.

"Mom, I'll have enough money to pay for you to stay home if you can help with Taylor temporarily. You can quit your job."

Mom had been working at a grocery store deli, on her feet all day. She complained about it constantly—I knew she desperately wanted to make a change. This was the first time I was able to support her in a meaningful way that made her life easier. I felt empowered. We agreed it would be best if I brought Taylor to stay with her while I was travelling. A few days later, I flew with Taylor to Mom's and got her settled into a new school. Finally, things were falling into place again. I was aware of what Einstein meant when he said,

"There are only two ways to live your life.

One is as though nothing is a miracle.

The other is as though everything is a miracle."

Life had suddenly become miraculous. I viewed the world as my playground. I spent my days jetting around the Caribbean, having the time freedom to read, study, and enjoy the peace and security from my newfound financial windfall.

Our most valuable asset is our attention. Whatever we place our attention on grows and expands. Notice an area of your life that is not where you want it to be and begin to focus your attention on what you want vs. what you don't. Once you are clear on what you want, your intention for the future, use high frequency emotions to raise your vibration. Gratitude, appreciation, enthusiasm are all renewable, high frequency feelings that will shift your energy and make you an attraction magnet for what you desire.

## *Chapter 28*

---

# LOVE IS A CHOICE
### ⸻ *1996* ⸻

A s the months went on, the excitement of travel began to wane. I loved scurrying from island to island, flying private, staring out the window into voluminous, puffy clouds. Even so, I missed my baby girl. I couldn't stay longer than a few days on my trips to Texas. Now in first grade, her chubby arms were beginning to thin out and she was losing the soft baby fat around her face. She'd gone from baby to little girl seemingly overnight. Although I was providing incredibly well for our little family, I wasn't there.

"Mommy please don't leave again," Taylor whined.

"Conchita Bambolita, Mommy has to work so I can get the *American Girl* doll you want for your birthday." "Okay, but promise me you'll be back soon."

"I will baby, make good choices for Nana."

I squeezed Taylor tight and reminded her she was the most important person in the entire Universe to me.

Heading out the door, I gave my mom a hug and thanked her for being a wonderful Nana. While beginning the hour-long commute from Terrell to DFW airport, a commercial came on the radio. I heard the words 'personal development', so I leaned forward, and turned the dial to raise the volume.

*The People's Network (TPN) is a brand-new television channel devoted to personal development in Dallas, Texas. We're recruiting salespeople looking to join a growing team!*

I sipped my coffee as I stared at the sea of brake lights ahead of me. I imagined myself not only consuming the personal development content I loved so much, but also being involved in its creation. I got excited at the thought of the many ways I might be able to take what I had learned and help others grow too.

That day as I hopped on board for my return flight from Grand Cayman, I found myself daydreaming about working for a company that would support my journey of self-realization.

TPN was a network marketing company, which meant I had to make an investment and would be my own boss. I would sell satellite dishes and subscriptions to the channel, mostly to friends and family, but also by cold calling. My passion for personal development helped me quickly climb the ranks in the company. I was goal-driven, action-oriented, and highly motivated. It wasn't long before the leaders in my market took notice.

One day, Bob and Sandy, my upline recruiters called me. Together, they sat in their office with me on speakerphone. Sandy asked, "So Jana, how would you feel about speaking at the weekly business briefing?"

My throat tightened. I suddenly flashed back to the Strawberry Queen pageant—*oh shit* echoed in my ears. "I can do that," I said, internally panicking. The panic was brief, however. In an instant, it dawned on me that this was an opportunity to practice public speaking. I knew I could make this opportunity work in my favor. I had become masterful at following my new credo: *fake it until you make it.*

Over the next few weeks, I practiced an inspiring speech focused on self-awareness, tenacity and creating a legacy through honoring your core values. My tone was encouraging and passionate, yet serious. I made it clear that miracles happen, but we hold the key to bringing them to life.

As prepared as I was, on the day of the event, my guts were in knots.

I took the stage; my hands quivering, my mouth dry and gave it my best. Midway through my speech, I froze when I caught the eye of someone in the front row. I became distracted, lost my train of thought and walked off stage. Although I was disappointed in myself, Bob and Sandy weren't deterred by my stage fright. Instead, they continued to coach me and encourage me to keep practicing so that I would gain confidence in my stage presence. Bob coached me to avoid looking into people's eyes, but rather to look at the middle of their forehead. That technique worked wonders. Regardless of my nerves, I pushed through and got up there again and again until being on stage began to feel like second nature. Over time, I became more comfortable on stage and became a leader for the company in South Florida.

It was during the first national convention I met Steve, a Texan, who was part of the executive leadership team of TPN. On the first night of the event, we stood at high-top tables socializing with colleagues. I noticed him right away as he conversed with others, listening intently. His demeanor was kind, his energy calm. He was older than I was, dressed in an elegant suit, his hair salt and pepper, slicked back. He had the kindest eyes I had ever seen in a man. He looked at me and smiled, his eyes catching the light. I smiled back with a sense of *knowing*. It was as if he was speaking to my soul through his gaze. I made my way through the crowd to him, reaching out my hand. "Hi, I'm Jana."

"I know who you are," he replied, his tone sweet. He took my hand in his—warm and soft. "I'm Steve."

Following the conference, we exchanged numbers and quickly became long distance friends. We would beep one another and sometimes send sweet notes via fax. We'd call one another during lulls in our day for quick catch ups and at night for longer conversations. I spent hours on the phone with him discussing philosophy, religion, and life. Steve was funny, he made me laugh. He had all these silly Texan sayings like, "this ain't my first rodeo" and when he spoke about people making lots of money he'd say, "they're in tall cotton" or if a woman was tall, he'd say, "she's a tall drink of water." I laughed a lot with Steve. What they say is true—laughter is the best medicine.

Our friendship was strengthening, but that was all it was to me. There simply was no romance for *me*.

On one of my visits to Texas, I met Steve for dinner. I sat across from him at a table in a loud, trendy restaurant, swirling my wine as he spoke. We knew each other so well at this point that we felt comfortable enough to share intimate details of our lives. As he spoke about life and what was going on with his kids, I began to feel curious about his past. I knew he had five kids from a previous marriage and had been divorced for some time, but I didn't know much about the actual breakup. I drew a breath and asked, "Steve, what was the reason behind your divorce?"

Without skipping a beat, he replied, "My ex-wife just stopped saying 'I love you'."

I tilted my head. "So, if she stopped saying 'I love you,' how did you handle it? What did you say to her?"

"I said what I always say. *Love is a choice*. We either choose love or we choose to close the heart and not allow it in."

As he spoke, the soft hum of conversation, clattering plates, and clinking glasses faded away. Shrouded in silence, things became crystal clear. I had been keeping my heart guarded from Steve's love. I had been focusing on his age, where he lived, his five kids, and his ex-wife. All of these things were excuses that kept me from really opening my heart to receive his love. With Steve, I hadn't felt the feelings I had previously felt in relationships; the butterflies, the intense desire to become intimate. Knowing this, I told myself that there wasn't a romantic connection between Steve and me. Now, in the soft light of the restaurant, I realized that I may have been wrong. Just like with Mom and Dad, and their parents before them, all my previous relationships started with fireworks and ended the same way. Being with Steve wouldn't be like that—no explosions, no huge, raucous fights.

Steve was open. He was attracted to me and wanted to provide for

Taylor and me, offering us a chance to settle down in ways we hadn't yet experienced. He was open and vulnerable about his feelings. I had never experienced a man being so open-hearted and emotionally available, not to mention the most important piece: he was spiritual like I was.

That night as we finished dinner, I'd decided. I would give a relationship with Steve a serious go. I viewed it as an extension of my mission to break cycles. I would finally allow myself to enjoy a stable relationship.

Just a few months later, Steve proposed to me. He had orchestrated a lovely dinner at a private supper club in Las Colinas outside of Dallas. He invited Mom, Taylor, and me. When we arrived at the restaurant, waiters in tuxedos and white gloves placed menus before us in unison. Each menu was personalized with his name, Steve Fleming, at the top. The food was perfectly cooked, decadent, and served with the utmost care.

After dinner, as we waited on dessert, Steve stood. We all stared up at him, quizzically until he spoke. "Janice, may I have the honor of marrying your daughter?" Mom smiled and nodded. He then turned to Taylor and asked, "Taylor, may I have the honor of marrying your mom? I would be honored to be your stepdad."

Taylor squealed with excitement. Mom beamed.

Steve then turned to me, bent down, and presented me with a beautiful ring and asked me to marry him. I took his hand and said, "Of course, I will."

Later that evening, when we were alone, I said, "Steve, you must know, I don't feel *in love* with you just yet. But I know I can grow to love you. You are a good man."

He smiled, took me in his arms and whispered, "That's good enough for me."

I was 30 years old when I married Steve, he was 43. It was a beautiful ceremony with 50 or so of our friends and family. With Dad out of my life, Roy walked me down the aisle. All five of Steve's kids were in the wedding, each playing their own special role. I loved seeing Taylor giggly and bubbly, tossing flowers as she walked down the aisle ahead of me.

My heart swelled as our families joined. Taylor sweetly hugged each one of her new sisters and her new brother. I was excited at the possibility of giving her a big family filled with love and support. However, there was one thing left for me to do for her.

Curt was still a proverbial thorn in our sides. He hadn't paid child support in many years and generally wasn't a stable presence in Taylor's life. I desperately tried to give Curt a chance to be in her life. But, it seemed, no matter how many chances I gave him, he could never give her what she deserved. The last straw occurred during a visit Taylor had with Curt and his parents, just after the wedding. Her very first night away, Taylor called me crying. "Mommy, I want to come home. Daddy's drunk. I'm scared. Can you come get me?"

I immediately jumped in my car for the three-and-a-half-hour trip from Dallas to Curt's parents' house in Oklahoma. On the way back to our house, I watched as tears rolled down Taylor's cheeks. She shared that her dad drank vodka the entire time and yelled at her and her cousins. It was clear to me that Curt was spiraling into the abyss of his addiction. I'd never spoken ill of Curt to Taylor, no matter what I knew about him. On the drive home, I made it clear to Taylor that if something happened to me, she would have to live with her daddy. I told her, "If you don't want that to happen, you can decide to let Steve adopt you. How do you feel about that?" She nodded and said softly, "I would like that." I made sure she knew that I loved and supported her no matter how she wanted to move forward.

With the stability I was enjoying with Steve, I had time to research the process of adoption. I was informed by the courts that in order to proceed, Curt would have to relinquish his parental rights. Since Curt was completely irresponsible and non-responsive to my calls, I reached out to his parents. Not knowing if they knew, I shared with them that Curt hadn't consistently been paying me the $400 a month in child support ordered by the court.

"If Curt wants to be active in Taylor's life, he'll need to be working an active AA or NA program and pay me the $15,000 in arrears he owes me."

"We are not responsible for his debts," his dad hissed. "Furthermore, we have advised him to just sign off on the adoption and say good riddance to you."

I was devastated for Taylor—yet I knew it was for the best. I had taken a massive step towards letting go of a dark past, and stepping into a bright, new future as a family with Steve.

It was almost a year after our wedding when the adoption was finalized—she was now officially Steve's daughter. On the day the process was complete, we picked Taylor up from her third-grade class and took her to dinner to celebrate her new name.

"You will always have your daddy, that will never change." I reminded her. "Now you just have two daddies and a new last name!"

"I never liked having a different last name than you anyway," she smiled.

## Chapter 29

# JUPITER
### ～ *1997* ～

I sat outside in my favorite chair, staring at the horizon. I glanced over at Steve whose eyes were gently closed as the sound of the waves washed over us. The sky was a dusty purple, the gulls screaming as they swooped and swirled above the water's surface. I sipped my white wine and let myself feel deep gratitude. This beautiful home on the water was our place of solitude. A few months earlier, we'd officially made the move from Texas to Jupiter, Florida. I had fallen in love with the town when I visited with my granny. She'd brought me to the Burt Reynold's Dinner Theatre, while I lived with her. Jupiter is a small seaside community filled with professional golfers, boaters, and lots of snowbirds. We'd enrolled Taylor in Jupiter Christian School and were enjoying living by the ocean.

Steve and I were building a successful business in network marketing. TPN was acquired by a company called Prepaid Legal (PPL) which later rebranded to LegalShield. In the first two years with PPL we earned 'millionaire club' status and became nationally known in the company. Due to our success, we were invited to speak to more than twenty-five thousand people at the annual convention in Las Vegas every year. We took

Taylor to Europe, spent summers and winters in San Miguel de Allende, Mexico, where Taylor would enroll at the Instituto de Allende and learn art, sculpture, and language. Steve was jovial and fun loving and never met a stranger. I was the serious one. I never quenched my thirst for a deeper spiritual connection, and I still craved passionate love. Even now as I looked over at Steve, the backdrop of our lives flanking his face, I just couldn't will myself to feel it. No matter how much money or how many peak experiences we gathered as a couple, I was often angry and sad. Adding insult to injury, integrating life with his five kids was hard—sometimes impossible. His ex-wife was always creating drama, finding ways to make even mundane things difficult. The older girls were hard for me to connect with as a parent figure. After all, I was only eleven years older than his oldest daughter and didn't know how to parent teenagers and young adults. I became a step-grandmother at 34. It all felt wrong. I felt like I was living a life that wasn't mine.

Steve was always pulling on my energy, wanting to be intimate. The more needy he became the more I pulled away. He monitored my email account and interrogated Taylor about my whereabouts. One time she asked me, "Mommy why does Daddy keep asking me if you talk to the mailman?" I was so tired of being accused of cheating, I finally just did it. One evening out with some girlfriends at a bar, I hooked up with my hair-dresser and slept with him that night. The next day, I left my computer open for Steve to see the emails I'd sent to my girlfriend discussing the infidelity. I hated myself for cheating but would have hated myself more by hiding it. I learned a valuable lesson; when we cheat on our partner, what we're really doing, is looking to others for love rather than giving it to ourselves. I wasn't honoring little Jana; I was cheating her out of what she deserved—my love. The fact was, she was unhappy because I was putting everyone else's happiness above my own.

My deeper hunger was for a career that was all mine. I needed purpose and connection to the things that lit me up. I reasoned if I couldn't fall in love with Steve, I'd focus as much time and energy as I could on building something for myself—something that was truly mine, not *ours*.

After years of trying, it was clear that I wouldn't be getting my formal degree. I abhorred math and couldn't get through the core curriculum with passing grades. Eventually, I threw in the towel on traditional education altogether and focused my attention on learning more about the things that inspired me.

My friend, Beth, heard about a spiritual symposium happening in Miami and asked me to join her. Within a few days we'd gotten tickets and booked a room.

When we arrived at the hotel, the energy was electric. I loved being among people who were as spiritually open as I was, hungry for knowledge and inspiration. As I perused the lists of authors and teachers from all over the world who would be doing breakout sessions, I noticed a teacher I hadn't heard of before: Debbie Ford. Her session was on a topic I'd read about but had a hard time learning—Jungian Shadow work. I stared at her bio—I had no idea how I hadn't heard of her before. She'd been on Oprah and her book, *The Dark Side of the Light Chasers*, had gone to number one on the New York Times bestseller list.

That afternoon, Beth and I sat in the sprawling conference room along with 600 other attendees. The lights dimmed and spotlights came up as Debbie walked out on stage and, as the applause died down, she said, "Hi, I'm Debbie Ford and I am a bitch!"

A smile burst across my face—I'd never heard anything remotely like this at a spiritual conference, and I'd been to dozens at this point. Debbie strutted across the stage smiling, taking in the applause. "I don't like her," Beth leaned over and whispered.

I, on the other hand, was hooked.

The lights illuminated the stage as Debbie said, "All right, now I would like you all to introduce yourselves to the person next to you with two words that describe your best qualities."

I shifted in my seat, turned to my left and said to the woman next to me, "Hi, I'm Jana, and I'm warm and friendly."

The room filled with nervous chatter punctuated by big, bubbly bursts of laughter. Debbie then signaled for everyone to quiet down and said,

"Now, introduce yourself to that same person with the opposite qualities you possess."

My mouth became dry as I looked at this stranger and said out loud what I didn't want anyone to know about me, "Hi, I am Jana, and I am cold and bitchy."

The rest of the workshop was intense, lighting me on fire for the concept of shadow work. Debbie led us through a series of exercises that helped us get in touch with the part of ourselves Carl Jung called The Shadow Self—the qualities we deny, disown and repress. Thanks to Debbie, this heady concept was starting to make sense to me.

Over the next few days, Beth and I attended lectures from experts, including Marianne Williamson, Maya Angelou, Eckhart Tolle and Wayne Dyer. Although each speaker's subject was fulfilling in some way, my heart and mind kept returning to Debbie. I knew I needed more.

It wasn't long after the conference wrapped up that I was traveling to San Diego to attend one of Debbie's *Shadow Process* workshops; a deep-dive weekend intensive into revealing and working with our shadows.

On the first day of the workshop, we were asked to find the qualities we would *never* want anyone to know about us; to identify the most hurtful thing anyone could say about us. I thought back on my childhood, picturing myself sitting at the dining table in front of my homework asking, "Mom, what's *white trash?*"

When I allowed myself to think about how long I'd struggled with this label, my heart sank. I thought about all the times this label prevented me from knowing that I was good enough; that I was wanted. It all started with those two words: *white trash*.

Debbie instructed us to stand in groups, expose our dark shadows, and participate in a mirroring exercise that forced each of us to face these qualities head-on. I stood with my group and steeled myself as three participants stared at me and called me white trash, slut, and bitch over, and over, and over again. I was amazed by the fire this exercise sparked. I felt my resistance to these labels loosening their tight grip—the labels that owned me for my entire life up to that point. It was liberating.

During our lunch break, a woman from Denmark came up to me and asked me to describe *white trash*. She said she had never heard the phrase in her country. The story that immediately came to mind would have been a perfect *Jerry Springer* episode. "Well, when I was sixteen, my mom concocted a plan to upgrade our single-wide trailer to a brand-new double-wide." "Oh," the woman said, leaning in interested. I continued, "Yep. Mom and her friend, Buddy Graves orchestrated burning down the old trailer to get the insurance money." "What? Isn't that arson?" the woman asked in disbelief. "Yeah, that's what white-trash does when they want a new trailer and can't afford it – just burn it down!"

After working with the dark parts of our psyche we were instructed to turn to the light. The qualities I was guided to own and embrace were *pure* and *innocent*. As I sat with my group and began repeating, "I am pure and innocent." I burst into tears. Memories flashed in my awareness, revealing the times in my life where I was anything but *pure* and *innocent*. The times I had been promiscuous. The times I didn't value myself. I had an epiphany in that moment; my real work would be embracing and integrating the Truth of my Essence. It was easy to believe I was white trash, a whore, or a bitch, but believing I was *pure* and *innocent* would take practice.

As the workshop continued, and Debbie worked with us to shed light on these shadows, I couldn't believe the inner shifts I was experiencing. I was bringing to the light the qualities I'd spent a lifetime hiding or rejecting. I had wasted an enormous amount of time and energy worrying what others thought about me.

During the next session, Debbie opened the floor for questions. I raised my hand and asked, "How can I work on not caring what other people think of me?"

Debbie laughed, then stared into my eyes and responded, "You only care what people think of you Jana if you agree with them. If you don't agree with them, what they think of you wouldn't affect you."

Hearing that, time stood still. My entire perspective shifted. I understood that I had the power to either accept myself or continue to judge myself. If I found myself concerned that others were judging me, I could use that as a reminder to check in with Little Jana and accept her exactly as she is.

## Chapter 30

---

# FAREWELL

*2000*

I stared out the window of our condo over the snow-capped peaks, which glistened in the morning light. I clutched my coffee cup in two hands and took a long, slow sip, glancing over at Steve as he finished his breakfast. I moved to the couch, sat down, and quickly found myself drumming my fingers on the side table. Despite the beauty of Vail, the exhilaration of the slopes, the decadence of dinners overlooking the mountains, I simply couldn't relax. There was something within me that felt restless—a nagging feeling that wouldn't leave. Something felt *off*.

I put my coffee down, grabbed the phone, and dialed Mom to make sure all was well with Taylor. "We're perfectly fine," she chirped. "Have fun!"

As I hung up the phone, I wanted my shoulders to drop and the tension in my body to release, but it wouldn't. My intuition was screaming, "Something isn't right!"

I pushed the feeling aside and got ready for the day. Steve and I enjoyed several runs on the slopes, a light lunch, and spent quality time together reading by the fireplace, but nothing helped. The next day I was still feeling restless, I let myself settle into the truth: I was being guided to *leave*.

I booked an early flight home and left Steve in Vail to finish out the week of skiing. I scurried through the airport and onto the plane, my anxiety rising the entire flight. When I finally walked into my house, I bolted directly to the blinking answering machine, I hit the play button and heard a voice I hadn't heard since I was a teenager—my Uncle AJ, Dad's older brother. Uncle AJ was a slumlord. He had made his fortune owning trailer parks and selling mobile homes. He enabled Dad to stay an addict. When Big Momma died, he picked up where she left off. I didn't respect or like Uncle AJ. In a matter-of-fact tone, he said, "Hello, Jana Lee. I wanted to let you know that your dad passed away yesterday. Uh, call me back. Thanks. Bye."

I collapsed on the floor, letting out huge, heaving sobs. I pulled my knees into my chest and rested my head in my hands—I began to replay in my mind the last time I spoke with my dad. It was one year earlier when he called wanting to meet Steve and visit Taylor, whom he hadn't seen since she was a toddler.

"I'd love that, Dad." I said. "But only if I can speak with your AA sponsor first and confirm that you're working a sobriety plan. I'll be more comfortable that way."

The line went quiet, the tension built. He yelled, "You know what? When I die, don't come to my fucking funeral!" Then he hung up.

Those were the last words he ever spoke to me.

The next day, I called Uncle AJ back to ask about the funeral arrangements. Four days later Steve and I walked into the funeral home hand in hand. After we discussed specifics of what was to come, I asked Steve and the funeral director to leave me alone with Dad's body. As soon as I walked into the room, I gasped. His lifeless body had been so ravaged by alcoholism that I didn't recognize him. The only parts of him that seemed familiar were his hands. I walked over to him slowly, tears rolling down my cheeks.

In my hands, I held a letter and an old black and white picture of him holding me up in the air when I was a baby. In the letter, I wrote:

*Dear Dad, I know the last time we spoke, you said not to come to your funeral, but I felt you calling me, and I couldn't stay away. I forgive you for all the pain and suffering you caused me.*

*I forgive you for your anger.*

*I forgive you for leaving us so many times.*

*I forgive you for throwing me across the kitchen.*

*I forgive you for being so sick with addiction, that you couldn't be there for me.*

*Mom told me that she discovered you inappropriately touching me when I was a baby. It all made sense, the over-sexualization at a young age, and the fear I felt when left alone with you. I forgive you for that too.*

*I forgive you for the time you came home with $6,000 in cash from the insurance settlement. You spread it out on the coffee table and asked Roy and I to count out $1,000 each. You then said that we could keep it. We woke up the next morning, you were gone. The next time we saw you, you were broke.*

*I know you loved me the best way you knew how. I'm choosing to focus on the good. The memories of you singing to me and calling me Time Scallapucini. The drive-in movies, the silly accents. There was good in you Archie Lee Davis.*

*I will always love you.*

*Love, Time*

I reached down and pried apart his stiff, cold hands placing the letter and picture underneath. I leaned down and kissed his forehead. That's when I heard a sound from behind the casket. I looked up and saw a door that was previously shut, now open. I nervously looked around to see if someone was in the room with me – yet I didn't see anyone. In that moment, a swirl of warmth rushed through my body. I felt my daddy's arms wrapping me in the most beautiful, loving embrace. I closed my eyes. I heard him whisper:

*Thank you, Time, for coming.*

*I'm sorry I wasn't a good father.*

I felt my Daddy's spirit. Sobs arose from deep inside; Little Jana was mourning her Daddy.

I stood there as long as I could, basking in the feeling of my daddy's love. It was different than the love I'd always known from him. It was no longer forceful and conditional, it was gentle, accepting and timeless.

I turned to a stereo in the corner and placed a CD inside—Elvis', *He Touched Me* gospel album. The familiar sound of Elvis' soulful voice poured from the speakers,

*Amazing grace how sweet the sound*

*That saved a wretch like me*

*I once was lost, but now I'm found*

*Was blind but now I see*[14]

I placed the family photo album up on a pedestal for visitors to look through. Then I turned and looked at him once more. "I love you, Daddy."

I later learned through family members who were at Dad's bedside when he was in the hospital, that he had begged Uncle AJ to get ahold of me so I could get there to see him one last time. They said my uncle told Dad he didn't know how to find me. The truth was, he never tried. Yet, I felt Dad calling me all the way in Vail. He wasn't even close to perfect, but he was my Daddy, and I loved him just the same.

---

14  Elvis Presley, "Amazing Grace", RCA (1972)

## Chapter 31

# CALIFORNIA
### ❧ *2006* ❧

Over the next two years, I traveled back and forth from the East Coast to the West Coast, training with and learning from Debbie. In 2005, I was certified with a masters in integrative coaching from The Ford Institute at JFK University. Right away, I began leading women's retreats in Jupiter sharing all I had learned, focusing on synthesizing the psyche through shadow work. It was one of the most exciting times in my life. Leading retreats was new for me, but I was willing to take a leap and trust, knowing that this work felt like my dharma—my purpose in life. With each retreat I led, I became more comfortable with the role of being a teacher and sharing what I had learned in my own unique way.

At the last retreat I led in Jupiter, I had a very special participant. On the final evening, when everyone was sharing what they were taking away from the weekend, one of the ladies shared a story about a young single mother who she had worked with as a family therapist many years ago. She went on to say that she saw strength, intelligence, and leadership qualities in this young woman, that the young mother didn't yet see in herself. She ended by sharing that this weekend was a full circle moment for her. The teacher had become the student—it was Julie, the therapist I had worked with at Unity.

I felt overjoyed that she had come to the retreat in the first place. To be acknowledged by someone I respected and who had such a big impact in my healing journey felt like icing on the cake.

Within a year, Taylor graduated from high school, and I turned 40. I knew if I were to continue to grow, I needed to change my environment. I wanted to live somewhere new where I could continue to be challenged and uplevel my business.

At this point, Steve had partnered with Debbie, creating new products and working to sell her books and audios. I would volunteer as an assistant with The Ford Institute, assisting Debbie with her workshops and mentoring new coaches. Because of this, it made sense for Steve and me to move to California to be close to Debbie. We made the decision to move to Carlsbad, north of San Diego.

Though my relationship with Steve still lacked romance, I was focused. I had a career that gave me meaning and purpose. It felt like my life was finally becoming my own.

As I settled into the Ford community, I quickly began to see signs that something was off. The culture was unlike anything I'd ever experienced. Debbie had devotees all around her, constantly doting on her, often rubbing her feet and shoulders. The way she would allow the fawning, and sometimes encouraged it, was uncomfortable for me to watch.

During a break at a *Shadow Process* weekend, I approached her with a question. As I made my way toward her, she shooed the devotees away. When the room finally cleared, I asked, "Debbie, will this community love and accept me, even when I show up as my darkest self?"

She leaned forward, extending her arms, grabbing my face with her long, bony fingers and said, "Yes, Jana. I will love you even more."

I nodded my head and left the room, sending the devotees scurrying back, fawning over her once again. I looked back and furrowed my brow. The worship of this woman, the reverence, and the way she reveled in it was incongruent with the mission behind her work. Shadow work at its essence teaches us to own and embrace the projections we cast towards others; light and dark. Turning to walk away, the uncomfortable feelings remained within, but faded from my awareness. This was how things were at The Ford Institute, and now Steve and I were a big part of the organization. I didn't want to rock the boat.

Over the next few years, my relationship with Debbie and my time at the Ford institute grew more complicated. Although I saw the dysfunction for what it was, I had sipped the proverbial Kool-Aid. I couldn't help but seek to please, even dyeing my hair brown because Debbie didn't like blondes. At her direction, I stopped wearing makeup at the shadow process workshops and was instructed to "tuck my energy," otherwise, I'd be seen as attempting to take energy from Debbie. I was no longer an individual; I was a cog in the machine.

At the Institute, everything was so highly controlled, and feedback could only be received; never given back to Debbie or any member of her inner circle. The closer I became to the inner circle, the more I could see the fragility of it all. There were holes in the fabric that was holding it all together. I could see it, but I still couldn't break free from it. Regardless of what I was experiencing and what my intuition told me, I wanted her approval, I had placed her on the proverbial 'pedestal.'

In time, I thought back to the moment when I asked Debbie that fateful question—*Debbie, will this community love and accept me, even when I show up as my darkest self?* The answer should have had nothing to do with Debbie's undying love for me, a student. As a teacher now, my answer to that question to one of my students would be, "It doesn't matter if I love and accept you when you are your worst self—*will you?*" It took me several years of betraying myself in that community before I finally figured out what I needed to do. Forge my own path, step out of Debbie's *shadow* and continue seeking my highest truth.

Shadow work is taking 100% responsibility for your responses and reactions. The first step is observing when you are affected vs. informed. If you are affected it means you feel an emotional charge, either positive or negative towards something or someone. If you're affected it's evidence that a mirror is being held up to you, so you can see your own prejudices, judgments, and projections. Ask yourself, "What kind of person would do that"? This opens the door of awareness to the quality you are disowning, denying or rejecting within yourself. We all have the ability to possess every quality of character in the human experience. If you don't believe you could possess a quality you see in another, you're in denial and judgment. Shadow work leads us to forgiveness, compassion and acceptance of self, knowing that we can be everything 'sometimes'.

Make a list of qualities you dislike in others, and then ask yourself, have I been this way in the past, presently or possible future – or am I this way to myself? I've worked with countless people who truly claim they are not abusive, until they turn it on themselves. The relationship with self is the most important one you will ever have, and the one that all relationships mirror.

*Chapter 32*

---

# PARIS

❦ *2007* ❦

F all is one of the most beautiful seasons in Paris. The temperature is perfect, just warm enough for light clothing paired with a soft, oversize scarf. The light glistens, illuminating rows of historical buildings and long, sweeping cobblestone streets. The smell of fresh bread and delectable pastries swirls through the city, creating a fluttery feeling of home. Over one-hundred participants from all over the world gathered here, to learn about their shadows while enjoying a week-long cruise on the shimmering Seine River. During the day, I would assist in group sessions. During breaks, I'd spend time in lovely quaint towns getting a glimpse of the French countryside, before wandering the winding streets back to the boat. In these moments, navigating the cobblestone, flanked by busy cafés, I let myself feel the discomfort. Spirit was nudging me. I could feel it deep down, working its way into my consciousness, getting louder and louder. The still, small voice was becoming more urgent and insistent.

On the third day of the cruise, Debbie arranged for us to enjoy a Benedictine monk chant, at an austere abbey in Normandy. Part of the abbey was bombed during World War II and had been rebuilt. As we were waiting for the monks, my eyes wandered, taking in the simple, stark beauty of the abbey. The focal point of the room was a golden Christ on the cross, hanging from the ceiling. From time to time, slivers of light streamed through the windows, illuminating the figure and casting an ethereal glow around Christ's golden body. I looked at the crucifix, then at Debbie a few pews in front of me, I could no longer ignore Spirit's nudge.

I kept hearing this small voice within say, *"She is not your Source, I am."*

In a flash of inspiration, I knew what my next step would be. I would leave The Ford Institute and let go of the story that I needed to stay close to Debbie to have a successful career. I no longer felt the need to seek her approval. There, surrounded by holy relics of the past, I reconnected with the messages I'd heard long ago.

In the final days of the trip, it was as if the veil had been lifted. Debbie time and again confirmed the guidance I was receiving. She was hurtful and mean, constantly discounting me. One evening, as I sat in bliss after dinner, she strolled over with a look of contempt on her face. She said, "Jana, do you know what shadow you need to embrace?" placing her hand on her hip.

"No," I replied, waiting for the jab.

"You're an alcoholic, just like your dad."

Immediately, I was aware I wasn't affected by her words. My meditation practice had allowed me to refine my awareness, so that I wasn't triggered. I was informed; It was simply information. I was aware this had nothing to do with me. As she shared in her books, Debbie was the recovering addict. It was simply projection.

It was as if she could feel me pulling away and did everything she could to push my buttons. It seemed to me that Debbie was using my shadows and false belief of *not good enough,* to keep me dependent. I knew better, and Spirit was there to remind me that I had let go of that belief. I felt Grace time and time again when her words, intended to pierce my heart like a dagger, lost their power. I could only feel gratitude for the experiences, the opportunity to travel with her, and in the end, all of the lessons I had learned.

I hadn't led a group retreat since moving to San Diego. Upon returning from Paris, I began the plans for a group retreat in Santa Barbara, inviting all the women who knew me through my network marketing business. But before I could really devote my attention to my business, there was one crucial conversation I needed to have.

I hired a coach who had also been trained by Debbie but had left the organization a few years prior. Over the next few months, she coached me to have the courage to put in my resignation and to share my truth with Debbie. I made an appointment with Debbie by text, arranging for a phone call. She had affected positive change in my life, and I wanted to be sure I approached the conversation with respect and reverence for the teachings.

The conversation began cautiously but friendly enough. I shared about my desire to grow my own retreat business and my excitement about my upcoming Santa Barbara retreat with nearly eighty women registered. That's when the already tenuous conversation went awry.

"I feel grateful, I—"

Debbie cut me off, "Well, when are you planning to sign the non-compete and non-disclosure agreements?"

I took a deep breath, trying to regulate my emotions and steady my voice. "I'm not going to sign the documents. I'm leaving the Ford Institute."

*Deafening silence for what seemed like hours…*

When she finally spoke, in a menacing voice she said, "Jana, all you know, you learned from me."

I was shocked.

She continued, "You'll need to pay me ten percent of any earnings from your business."

My mind scrambled to make sense of what I was hearing. "Debbie, that would be like a university requiring anyone who graduated pay the institution royalties for life."

Silence again, the line disconnected.

It was one of the most difficult conversations I had ever had, and one that I felt I managed well. The time had arrived for me to take responsibility and fully step out on my own.

Within five years of my departure, Debbie Ford's body was laid to rest. She had kept hidden the fact she was diagnosed with stomach cancer a decade prior, after *The Dark Side of the Light Chasers* went to number one on the NYT Bestseller list. When she appeared on *Super Soul Sunday* with Oprah in 2012, she finally admitted publicly that she had been in remission and now the cancer had come back with a vengeance.

Regardless of the dysfunction in the community, I am incredibly grateful for Debbie and how she challenged me to face the dark parts of my psyche and embrace the light. Debbie's teachings taught me how to accept and love myself, even when I showed up in some of my least attractive qualities. I'd need to remember this as I continued my quest to seek out and love Little Jana and bring my unique gifts to the world.

*Chapter 33*

# THE CHOPRA CENTER
## ❧ *2008* ❧

I had to admit, having Taylor in college was complicated for me. I was so proud of my daughter, thrilled that she was taking this massive step in pursuing higher education. As I was slowly working on letting her go, some of my old demons surfaced. I'd think about her in school and feel like I was falling from a skyscraper – out of control. I'd flash back to my own experiences.

*Bursts of light at bars—up all night*
*Drunken nights*
*Stabbing, ripping pain in my throat*
*Pressure on my body*
*Pain*
*Lost*

Unable to stop the swirl, I would find myself spun out, wrestling with my own body to find peace. I was constantly reminding myself that Taylor wasn't me and she would be fine. One night when the panic threatened to carry me away, I called Debbie, and she told me to come over to her house in La Jolla. Together, we sat on her floor in front of the fireplace overlooking the beautiful Pacific Ocean, while I sobbed with my head in my hands. "I'm just so scared for her—I don't want her to have the same experiences I did."

Debbie leaned forward looking deeply in my eyes and said, "What quality is this bringing up for you?"

I knew instantly—it was a word I'd held onto and imposed on myself for many years—*whore.*

Debbie replied, "Yeah, Jana, a part of you is a whore. So, you must find the lesson and gifts of the experiences that made you judge and disown this part of yourself." She folded her hands in her lap and continued, "Think about what kind of mother you have been for Taylor because of your experiences."

I nodded as she reminded me that because I was objectified as a child and as a young adult, I did everything to protect Taylor from experiencing the same. A space opened in my mind, and I was able to see clearly that the experiences of being sexually exploited pushed me to want to create safety for Taylor. I left Debbie's house feeling calm and at peace.

Yet, the panic attacks continued.

I reached out to a traditional doctor who only wanted to prescribe Xanax and Zoloft. That didn't feel right to me. It was time to take the next step in my healing and all teachers kept saying the same thing—a meditation practice is imperative for the spiritual seeker who wants peace of mind. I hadn't stayed consistent with the practice from Taylor's early years living with my mom.

Just before my trip to Paris with Debbie, I began attending the Chopra Center at La Costa Resort, a mile away from my home in Carlsbad. I specifically wanted to learn mantra-based meditation and commit to a formal practice, which would help me regulate my nervous system.

After receiving my personal mantra and re-committing to a daily practice, I enrolled in the Primordial Sound Meditation teacher training and began a year long journey to become certified in the ancient teachings of Vedanta—non-dualism. I would learn from two of the world's most influential teachers and physicians, Dr. Deepak Chopra and Dr. David Simon.

Meditation became one of the most transformative practices of my life. I recognized that it was the meditation practice that allowed me to hear the voice of my soul during my trip in France. It was the stillness and silence that was allowing me to go deep and hear what Spirit had to say. Deepak called this, "eavesdropping on the mind of God." Meditation was also helping me connect more deeply to my Wise Little One, allowing me to hear what she was communicating. I could intuit what she wanted; I could feel what she needed. I became deeply committed to this practice, opening me up to greater peace and a deeper connection to Spiritual guidance.

As soon as I graduated from the program, I volunteered to teach meditation to Chopra Center guests. I was meeting people from all over the world, thriving as I built my retreat business. It was during this time that I started to feel homesick for a place I'd only lived for six months; somewhere that felt like my true home—Santa Fe, New Mexico. I longed to be beneath the big, blue sky, wandering the streets lined with terracotta pueblos that lit up as the sun set. I missed the expansive sky and vistas. This land called out to me—it was a place that felt holy. It was a place my heart needed, but something inside me sought confirmation. I'd been telling myself that I needed the credibility of working at the Chopra Center to build a more successful career, repeating the same thought pattern I had when I was at the Ford Institute.

One afternoon, Deepak was filming a segment for the Enlightenment Teacher Training the Chopra Center was creating. The filming was private—just a few teachers were invited to participate as the audience. Overall, everyone was quiet and respectful, although, before the filming started, one of the teachers came up to Deepak and asked for a photo with him. Vastly different from Debbie, he was visibly annoyed with this request. Both Deepak and Dr. Simon taught not to worship the guru. Deepak would advise "if someone is pointing to the moon don't worship the finger." I appreciated this perspective as I was still healing from being a part of the Ford community. As the house lights went down and filming began, I found myself mesmerized. I sat in the front row taking copious notes, soaking up every bit of the teaching I possibly could. During filming, Deepak received a phone call—it was Larry King. With the cameras no longer recording, Deepak paced the stage as he learned there had been a bombing in India. Larry invited Deepak to be a guest on the show that same evening in Los Angeles to speak about the impact of the events.

After the phone call, there was a short break. During that time, I scanned my notes, reviewing the wisdom Deepak had shared. As he came off stage, still engrossed in my notes, he approached me, touched my shoulder and said, "Would you like a photo together, Jana?"

My heart leapt; I nodded in agreement. As I stood and he placed his arm around me, I understood the message he was trying to send: "the most detached wins."

Synchronistically, I was flying out of San Diego airport in the wee hours of the morning, just a few days after that experience. It just so happened that Deepak and his wife, Rita, were at the airport too. Steve chatted with Rita while I spoke to Deepak.

"Where are you headed?" he asked.

I replied, "I'm heading to lead a retreat in Florida and further the teachings."

He smiled and said, "That's good."

As we loaded our things through security, I had a burning question I was preparing to ask Deepak, still struggling with how to formulate it. That confirmation—I was still seeking it, but I knew I had to phrase it carefully to Deepak. He wasn't one to weigh in on personal matters in such a direct manner.

Once through security, I saw him at Starbucks getting a coffee. I decided it was a perfect opportunity to approach him. "Deepak?" I said, touching his shoulder. "Excuse me, I have a question."

He kept his head down, stirring his coffee.

Now unsure of what to say, I stood there in his presence—silent.

He looked up at me and smiled. He said, "We're on the same plane."

Without any opportunity for more discussion, he walked away.

I was dumbfounded. What did he mean?

As I boarded the flight and sank into my seat next to Steve, I began to feel he may have known what I was going to ask him—*should I stay at the Chopra Center seeking greater credibility, or do I follow my heart and go back to Santa Fe and build my own business?* As I let my mind relax, I could feel it. My teacher's cryptic answer was letting me know something extraordinary. He was saying, "You don't need me. I am not your Source. We are on the same 'plane' consciously to make a difference in the world. Go do it!"

It was just the message I needed. I squeezed Steve's hand as the plane rumbled and began to hurdle down the runway. I knew then that I would return home and set in motion our move back to Santa Fe.

*Chapter 34*

# THE LAND OF ENCHANTMENT
## ⟳ *2010* ⟲

*I think New Mexico was the greatest experience from the outside world that I have ever had. It certainly changed me forever. The moment I saw the brilliant, proud morning shine high up over the deserts of Santa Fe, something stood still in my soul, and I started to attend … In the magnificent fierce morning of New Mexico, one sprang awake, a new part of the soul woke up suddenly, and the old world gave way to a new.[15]*
—From New Mexico by D. H. Lawrence

The words of the English author, D. H. Lawrence resonated powerfully within me. I felt like my roots plunged deep into the red soil and my soul took flight once I returned to New Mexico. This was my home. It was utterly different from living near the ocean. There was no salty breeze, no misty nights followed by cool, hazy mornings. Now, instead of walking along the water's edge, I was living in a state of

---

15  D. H. Lawrence, "New Mexico", Mornings in Mexico and Other Essays (Cambridge University Press, 1927)

deep, soul connection with the earth. This was a place where I'd spent days staring at mountains that jutted into the sky and nights marveling at the Milky Way. I would wander through the forest, the beautiful smell of minerals filling my nostrils. It was as if Mother Earth knew exactly what I needed now—my next layer of healing.

My marriage to Steve had finally run its course. After so many years together, I was worn down caretaking and nagging him constantly. I observed I was beginning to dislike myself in relationship with him. It was a high price to pay. Even though I focused on his good qualities and loved him, I just wasn't *in love* with him. It had become clear that our relationship wasn't improving, and that he and I were growing in different directions. Steve had started drinking more and more, and the respect I had for him and myself with him, were dwindling. He functioned, so I would tell myself, *its ok, he isn't an angry drunk like my dad. He is kind and loving. He makes me laugh.*

Simply put, I was in denial, lying to myself, betraying myself, and cheating on myself. I justified his behavior because, the truth was, I was scared as hell to leave him. In many ways I felt like a child when I married him—he stepped in to care for Taylor and me. I wondered how I'd be able to make it on my own. I would terrorize myself with worst-case future scenarios. I also feared Steve wouldn't be able to manage life without me. I worried constantly that leaving him would mean that he would fall apart. My heart told me; my intuition told me; Spirit told me that I was not responsible for Steve.

I couldn't hide my feelings anymore; fear and sadness were etched into my very being. Steve knew things were coming to an end. We had begun fighting about who would stay in the house if we dissolved the marriage—it had become a tug of war between us. In the turmoil, I kept asking for a sign that would reveal the path for me. It was during a retreat I was leading in Florida the Fall of 2012 when I got the call that Steve had been arrested for driving while intoxicated. The humbling event of being arrested and spending the night in jail was what woke Steve up. He knew the relationship was now over and that it was his responsibility to move out. Over the next month, we divided all our belongings. I rented a moving truck and drove from New Mexico to California to help him get settled in his new place. Although it was the end of our marriage, we both agreed we wanted to part consciously.

It would have been our eighteenth anniversary when we finalized our divorce. Steve flew to Santa Fe, we drove to the courthouse, signed the papers, filing everything without attorneys. That evening we dined at Geronimo, our favorite restaurant, and reminisced about the past and all we had experienced together. We were now divorced friends and would remain so.

I needed to get to the bottom of what kept me defaulting to codependent relationships. I desperately wanted to break the cycle once and for all. This is when I decided to leave the house I shared with Steve and move an hour and half north to Taos. It would be a fresh start.

Taos is an iconic Western town with a population less than 7,000. The town itself is small, filled with an ancient, permeating magic that creates a uniquely palpable energy. Adobe buildings line streets whose beauty shifts as the light changes throughout the day. The sleepy, dusty town sits at the base of mountains that burst forth, framed by a sky that fades into a shade of rose as night falls.

Most people in Taos remain on the fringe of society, preferring to live on the land, connected to nature, choosing solitude over keeping up with the Joneses. They live in homes called 'Earthships', set back from dirt roads, down winding paths that give way to big mesas. The large plots of land their homes sit on become their lifeline. They supply water, food, and a deep connection to Mother Earth.

After a short search, I found a house three-miles off a paved road, near the Rio Grande Gorge, a 950-foot crevice into the earth, like a mini-Grand Canyon. The house was in such a remote location that sometimes I would get snowed in for days due to winter conditions. I'd bundle up with several layers, pull on my tall work boots and zip my down jacket up to my chin before heading out into the frigid mountain air. Keeping the house warm with propane was expensive, so I'd chop native pinon and cedar wood, feeling like a pioneer from a past life surviving the harsh winter. After building a fire in the kiva fireplace, I'd bundle up with my journal and cry as the fire crackled and popped. Despite the challenges I faced with Steve, I missed having a partner. I would stare into the fire, my mind raging alongside the flames, flooded with images and stories: *Desperate. Old. Alone. Just like my mother.*

My business was suffering. I wasn't in a place to be authentic. I felt like an imposter when I was working with clients. Certainly, if what I was teaching worked, my life would represent it. I needed to slow down and take this opportunity to begin again.

During this time, I returned to beginners' mind. I recalled reading a passage in a Zen Buddhism book: *"In the beginner's mind there are many possibilities. In the expert's mind there are few."*

I was now in a place to midwife the parts of myself that I needed to strengthen and embody. The old stories rooted in my childhood continued to hold me back. It was time to peel back more layers and continue healing. I returned to inner child work and found a teacher that had a simple system, teaching students to relate to their feelings like they would with a young child. If I was feeling a painful emotion, I would imagine Little Jana was the part of me that was feeling that way. This allowed me the space to work with the feeling and understand where it was coming from. I learned that there are some painful feelings that are an inevitable part of the human experience. Feelings such as grief, helplessness over others, fear in present danger—they all arise in response to external events. Most of the painful emotions we experience are a result of the meanings we assign to those events. I was re-parenting Little Jana, unwinding the conditioning of the parenting I received from Mom and Dad.

The thing about growth is, it's never ending. I withdrew from the world for weeks, completely focused on myself, giving Little Jana my undivided attention. Whereas I once sat in front of the mirror and felt repelled by the concept of looking myself in the eyes, I now spent days looking in the mirror, facing all my shadows and false beliefs. I was mirroring back to myself everything I was thinking and believing that was limiting me. One evening, it dawned on me that I desired a man who was affluent and wealthy. So, I headed to the bathroom and looked into the mirror and began processing the worst judgment I had about women who marry for money. "You're a gold digger. I am a gold digger." I repeated these words over and over, feeling repulsed by that part of myself. As I continued to expose the shadow of gold digger, it lifted. I felt lighter and began to laugh at myself. I heard the Kanye West and Jamie Foxx hit, "Gold Digger" in my head. I picked up my phone finding the song and turned it up loud. I danced around the house singing and laughing. It's important to not take ourselves so seriously. Deepak always said, "seriousness is a sign of self-importance, enlightenment is about *lightening up*."

I took long hikes down into the gorge and would sit on the riverbank of the Rio Grande with my dogs, clearing my mind and enjoying the simplicity of life. I would sit to meditate during the afternoon and come out of my practice and it would be dark—I'd have spent hours gone. Slowly, I was beginning to come back to life, caring for a part of me that needed me most.

When I was ready to venture out again, I did so slowly. It wasn't long before I met what Elizabeth Lesser's book, *Broken Open* describes as my 'shaman lover'. A man who was an amalgamation of all the wounds from my childhood and all men I had allowed in my life, based on that primary relationship with my dad. After so much time alone, I opened my life to Jake quickly. After all, he was familiar.

Jake was a musician, spiritual seeker, nature lover, and a yogi. Over the next two years, he tore my heart open and revealed to me how unworthy I still believed I was. He was chaos. He showed me the parts of myself that still needed integration. It took me nearly two years of on again off again drama to get the lessons.

The relationship reminded me of another long-held false belief I held, *getting love from others feels better than giving love to myself.*

It was a lightbulb moment.

Two years into the relationship. Jake and I were in Kauai, at a café in Hanalei Bay, getting sandwiches. The girl behind the counter told him he had to put a shirt on to be served. He looked at her, his cheeks pink, his teeth gritted together and responded, "Go fuck yourself."

Humiliated by his behavior I looked down.

That's when she whispered to me under her breath, "You can do so much better than that guy."

Her words stung. Here was this pimple-faced teenager with hickeys on her neck, offering me, an emotional healing teacher, advice on my love life. Yet, although her words jabbed at me, I knew they were true. It was the soul slap I needed, and Spirit used the perfect teacher to give me this lesson. I had been abandoning Little Jana again, afraid to be alone. This teenager was right, I deserved better. I walked out of the sandwich shop a different person.

I was ready to come back to the world, and not hide anymore. I packed up a moving truck, left Taos, and moved back to Santa Fe. As if all was orchestrated, I quickly found a lovely home on five acres on the outskirts of town. My business began to grow again, and before long, I was booked months out for private retreats. Each day, I would gaze into the mirror and ask my Wise Little One, Little Jana what she wanted to do, what she wanted to wear, and even what she wanted to eat. She was my guide. I was her protector.

## *Chapter 35*

# SCRIPTED

### ❧ *2015* ❧

K nown as monsoon season, summer in Santa Fe is captivating. Massive, dense, dark-gray thunderclouds form as the day warms, then colossal raindrops cascade from the sky each afternoon, dropping the temperature ten degrees or more. After the intensity of the storms, the wind calms, the clouds become bright white again, brilliant rainbows color the Eastern skies. The land is covered in clusters of vibrant yellow Chamisa and fields of bright sunflowers that burst like gilded fireworks.

Summer is the time I claim for Little Jana—taking time off to let her play and explore. One morning, I left the house with my rescue fur babies, Kiley and Bonita. We headed to the Santa Fe National Forest for a hike. My inner child loves to run free on the trails, ducking behind trees before exploring the mountain creeks, looking for fairies.

I carried a blanket in my backpack with me as I hiked, my dogs bounding ahead excitedly as I made my way. When I spotted a small clearing, I called them to my side as I spread my blanket on the soft forest floor. I chewed on a handful of almonds as I laid back, staring through the aspens at puffy clouds, lazily passing over the brilliant turquoise sky. The earth smelled like pine and cedar.

*I am safe.*

*I am exactly where I am meant to be.*

I closed my eyes, sunlight speckling my face as my dogs curled up nearby. Soft birdsongs swirled with the distant sounds of branches moving in the breeze as I began to transport myself to my ideal future, using my imagination to create every detail.

I am laying here with a man beside me—my beloved. I wiggle closer to him resting my head on his shoulder as he tucks his hands behind his head. He whispers, *I am so inspired by you.*

I nuzzle my head into the crook of his arm.

*You have brought so much peace, love, and joy into my life.*

I smile.

I jump at the sound of a big boom of thunder in the distance. It is time to head back down before the monsoons arrive. I look over at my beloved. He scurries to his feet and reaches down to help me up. He folds the blanket and tucks it into my backpack, which he slings onto his back. I call the dogs and, together, we bound down the mountain. Just as we reach the base, fat drips of rain begin to make their way through the branches and plop onto the soil beneath our feet. Laughing, we run through the rain like kids, soaked by the time we reach the car. My beloved pulls me close and takes my face in his hands. He kisses me.

*I love you.*

My imagination continues to dance. It's getting late. The sun is slipping below the horizon, leaving the sky a creamy shade of rose. We are now in my kitchen preparing a meal. I stand at the stove as he turns up the volume on the music—Diana Krall's velvety voice diffuses through the house. He comes up behind me and kisses my neck as I stir the pot of soup. Once I ladle it into bowls, we sit across from one another and talk about the future we are building together. My heart swells and I feel my body rush with that warm sensation of gratitude. At that moment my body and brain don't know the difference between my thoughts and reality. He stands and walks around the table, offers me a hand, and pulls me into him.

*We dance.*

My eyes fluttered open just as my body relaxed against his. I stared once again at the brilliant blue sky and held onto the feeling of gratitude. The feeling of positive expectancy. The feeling of him. I sat up and gathered my things, signaling the dogs to follow.

As I made my way home, the skies darkened, and great bolts of lightning and thunder rolled through the lush green mountains. I felt connected to myself, grounded, relaxed, and content, promising to forever honor myself—Little Jana—so that when my beloved did show up, I would be secure within.

My relationship with myself was solidifying.

*Giving love to myself feels better than getting it from others.*

This new belief was taking root and blossoming. It was helping me understand that I was whole. I didn't need to find my beloved. But, if I did, I'd be ready. For the first time in my life, I was feeling stable and grounded—alone. And it felt amazing. I decided it was time to do something I had dreamed of for many years. I booked a trip—a meditation retreat at The Esalen Institute in Big Sur.

The power of our imagination is miraculous. We can make thought and mental images as real as what we are experiencing. In fact, the brain doesn't know the difference between a thought and an actual experience. Whatever you are desiring to manifest in your life, first, make a list of all the things you don't want and on the opposite side of the column make a list of what you do want. This helps you gain clarity on your hearts desires. Once you have completed the 'do want' list, use it to write clear intentions with elevated emotions. An example would be, "When I envision managing challenging situations in a calm, clear and coherent way I feel empowered."

*Chapter 36*

# A FATEFUL MEETING

❧ *2015* ❧

I shifted in my seat and cracked the window as I crossed the city limits into San Jose. My heart was full—I was in the same city as my daughter. Taylor had moved here with a boyfriend a few years prior. That relationship resembled what she had witnessed between Steve and me. However, Taylor figured out it wasn't a healthy relationship for her, much more quickly than I did, ending it before things got ugly. She was thriving now; she turned her passion for health and nutrition into a career as a private personal trainer. She had met her future husband, Travis, who was also a personal trainer. Travis was everything a mom would want for her daughter. Besides being 6'4", muscular and handsome, he was funny, polite, well-mannered and respectful. I looked forward to seeing them.

I pulled into the parking lot of Trader Joes, slid out of the car, grabbed a cart nearby, and pushed it inside. The ice-cold air, the people scurrying from aisle to aisle, the hum of chatter, all felt foreign after so many days of meditation and quiet. Quickly, I made a mental list of things I wanted to bring Taylor, grabbing them one by one: steaks, fresh fruits and vegetables, snacks, and treats for Lucky, her rescue puggle. I moved on autopilot, my mind still churning. I thought about the crystal-clear voice that said, *leave*, the immediate disappearance of symptoms of illness I'd felt, the deep connection to Little Jana, Jonathan the seagull – all the signs.

I rushed out of the store, jogged through the parking lot, then piled the groceries into the back seat. Back in the car, I headed toward Taylor's apartment. Fall was beginning to creep in, offering swirls of reds, yellows, and pinks. The street leading up to Taylor's apartment complex was lined with crimson Japanese Maples, standing at attention as if to usher me to her doorstep. When I drove through the gate and pulled into the parking spot outside her door, she ran to the car, her long blond hair bouncing with each step. "Mom!" she called.

Like Dad had with me, I had many silly pet names for Taylor: Lucy, Rooney, Conchita-Bambolita, Rae-Rae. I opened my arms, and she dove into them. I wrapped her into a tight hug. "Hi, Conchita!"

Travis stood in the doorway, clutching Lucky who was panting and snorting, begging to get down and run to me. I grabbed the bags and carried them inside, greeting Travis and Lucky as I went.

"Mom! You didn't have to do this—thank you!" Taylor said as we walked over the threshold into her apartment. I loved being there and seeing how well she was doing to take in the life she'd created for herself. Taylor's home felt like her—warm, orderly, filled with love. Together, we unpacked the groceries while chatting about her plans for a Christmas visit, and I told her about my experience at Esalen. I looked at my phone. It was time to head to the airport. Taylor and I exchanged hugs and kisses, then I left heavy hearted, but happy.

Less than thirty minutes later, I was pulling my suitcase through San Jose airport, the wheels gliding across the pristine floor. Once I got to the gate, I sat down and intentionally took a few deep breaths, centering myself. The past few days had been such a whirlwind, but I knew I was being led. All I had to do was keep myself centered, breathe, listen, and flow. I walked onto the plane with a steady resolve and a strong connection to Spirit and Little Jana. I stared out the window as we ascended into the clouds.

*Leave*
*Giant Redwoods*
*A Seagull*

In contrast to the cooler temperatures in California, the weather in Las Vegas was still hovering in the mid 90s. I gazed out the window as the plane slowly descended, the flashing lights of the strip clearly visible, even from the air. When the tarmac came into view, waves of heat rippled above the black tar, a mirage of hundreds of pools of water. As we pulled into the gate and passengers began to stand and file out, I made my way off the plane. As soon as I walked out of the breezeway and into the airport, I winced. Robotic sounds of jingles, clanks, beeps and brief melody clips slashed at my senses, the sound of hundreds of slot machines in action. I dug into my bag and rooted around for my noise cancelling headphones. I turned the volume up with calming spiritual music to drown out the noise pollution. I stepped into a nearby shop and grabbed a water and some nuts and paid the attendant before heading to my gate. The music soothed me as I allowed my mind to return to Carmel and the night before. I could see it so clearly—I could see myself through the eyes of Little Jana. Through the lens of her gaze, I saw my gait, observed my slow, steady breaths, reveled in my own strength. What I saw through her eyes was remarkable. Strong feelings of contentment washed through me.

*I am all I truly need.*

*The Universe has my back.*

I sat at my gate, swigging water and staring out the window, gazing over the cityscape. This was the place of my conception. Visions of Mom and Dad danced in my mind, their seductive love, dangerous, and volatile. I pictured their fights, how vividly I could recall them, yet how distant they felt now. From this place of peace and self-love, that part of my past felt muffled, buried under by new memories, awareness, and healing. I placed my hand on my heart.

Softly, I whispered, *I love you*.

I looked away from the window just in time to notice the flight attendant standing at the counter making an announcement. A line had already formed, and people had begun shuffling onto the plane. Since I'd booked my last-minute trip on Southwest, I knew what that meant. I'd be stuck in a middle seat. Group C, number 42. One of the last to be called.

As I boarded the plane still wearing my headphones, I turned the corner and made eye contact with a handsome man sitting in the bulkhead row. He had bright eyes and dark brown hair tinged with silver, cut short and neatly styled. Our eyes met, but he quickly looked away. I felt it inside—an instant attraction. The seat next to him was empty so I asked, "Is this seat available?"

"Yes," he replied shyly, standing up.

I loaded my things into the overhead compartment and noticed that the woman by the window couldn't get her seatbelt around herself. I turned and quietly asked the flight attendant for a seatbelt extender and slipped it to the woman without a word. She smiled and thanked me with a nod.

I settled into my seat and pulled out my yoga teacher manual. I opened it and began reading. I had enrolled in yoga teacher training with a teacher I had dreamed of training with, Saul David Raye, a few months prior and was preparing for my next two week residential in Ojai, California. I glanced over at the guy sitting next to me—he was reading a book about happiness.

*Poor guy,* I thought. *He needs to read a book about how to be happy.*

Pretending to read my manual, I stole several looks at the man, noting his brows, which were knitted together, and his eyes that had a faint red tint to them. I wondered if he'd lost money in Vegas and was feeling emotional, or whether he was just having a bad day. Eventually, I turned back to the manual, and he shut his book and closed his eyes, leaning back on the headrest. The flight to Albuquerque is a little more than an hour. It wasn't long before the pilot made an announcement of the local time and temperature and asked the flight attendants to prepare the cabin for landing. I closed my manual as the man sat up and adjusted his seat. He looked over at me, pointed to the tattoo on my forearm and said, "That's beautiful. What does it mean?"

I self-consciously pulled my arm into my chest and said, "That's personal." I have my mantra tattooed on my left forearm.

"I'm so sorry," he said, looking away.

"I'm kidding," I said with a laugh. "It's my mantra."

"Oh," he said with a nod, his eyebrows raised.

"Do you meditate?" I asked.

"I do," he replied. "Hi, I'm Lance."

"I'm Jana, nice to meet you," I responded.

That began the next thirty-minutes of deep sharing. As the plane descended, Lance shared that he was separated from his wife and that they were preparing for divorce. He'd be moving into a new place as soon as he got home. He was sad, I was right.

"This morning was one of the most painful times of my life. I got up knowing that I'm leaving my two teenage boys. I feel like a failure, I—" he paused, then tilted his head. "Do you always have deep conversations like this on airplanes, because I've never had this experience?"

I smiled and said the first thing that popped into my head, "My motto is 'go deep or go home.'"

He laughed. We caught each other's eyes for a brief second. In that instant, I found myself breathless. An electric shiver ran down my spine. I hadn't felt anything like this for so many years. Yes, there was physical attraction, but it was more than that. Something deeper. Something layered. Something fated.

As the plane landed, bouncing slightly on the runway, Lance shared that he was a physician interested in mind/body health practices and stress reduction. He asked me the name of my business and I quickly handed him my business card. As soon as we reached the gate, the plane erupted into a flurry of activity as passengers grabbed their bags and hurried off the plane. I flew out of the plane and rushed into the bathroom to touch up my makeup before catching up with him.

As I came out of the bathroom, I quickly looked from left to right, then began walking back toward the gate. Lance was nowhere in sight. I began running through the airport, aware that I would be mortified if he turned around and saw me running to find him, but I wanted to see him again and say a proper goodbye. I jogged to the escalator as I descended.

There he was.

I was out of breath and didn't want to appear frazzled, so I steadied myself before I reached his side and said coolly, "Hey, there you are!"

He turned and said, "Oh, where'd you go?"

"Bathroom," I replied.

"Ok, well," he said, holding my gaze. "Have a safe trip back to Santa Fe."

My heart dropped a little as he walked toward the exit, pulling his suitcase behind him. I raised my hand and offered a small wave, "Bye."

Although a part of me seemed to want more from Lance, for him to ask me to have coffee and continue our deep conversation, I was able to turn within and comfort myself.

*All is well—I love you.* I silently said to Little Jana.

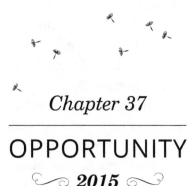

*Chapter 37*

---

# OPPORTUNITY

❧ *2015* ❧

*There is some kiss*
*we want*
*with our whole lives.*[16]
—Rumi

The doors slid open, and I walked outside into the dry, warm Albuquerque air. The shuttle to the parking lot pulled up in front of me, and I stepped inside, my mind still dancing over the conversation with Lance and the way I felt as we spoke.

As the shuttle made its way through the sea of cars, my phone began to ring. I pulled it out of my bag and, noticed it was my toll-free number for my business. I cleared the call, planning to return it as soon as I was at my desk. I wondered if it might be Lance since it was a 505 area-code number.

---

16  Rumi, The Essential Rumi, ed. Coleman Barks (Harper Collins, 1995)

Finally at my car, I placed my bags in the backseat and eased myself in behind the wheel. I let the silence hold me, closing my eyes for a moment, feeling peace with my decision to come home. The engine roared to life, and I began the hour-long drive up to Santa Fe, the gritty landscape and jutting mountains offering a warm welcome.

As soon as I arrived home, I poured myself a cup of tea and settled behind my desk. I'd been away for several days and knew I'd have a pile of emails to weed through, so I figured I'd tackle them one-by-one. As the glow of the screen lit up my face, my lips burst into a smile. There, at the top of my inbox, was an email from Lance. The subject: opportunity.

*Jana, I don't know that I believe in fate, but I do believe in opportunity, and I would like the opportunity to get to know you better.*

*–Lance*

A wave of excitement rushed through my body, my heart began to race, I was giddy.

I quickly replied,

*I like opportunists. I would welcome getting together.*

*–Jana*

Six nights after we met on the plane, I arrived at the restaurant where we'd agreed to meet. I felt excited and confident as I closed the door of my car and made my way through the parking lot, my heels clicking on the rutted asphalt. As I approached the entrance, I smiled seeing Lance waiting for me, holding the door open. In his left hand, he held six roses wrapped in plastic wrap with wet paper towels cradling the stems. His hands were shaking as he handed them to me. "These are from my garden."

I tipped them toward my nose. Their beautiful fragrance filled my being. "They're beautiful," I smiled.

The hum of other dinner guests faded into the background as we were ensconced in our own little world. Just as it was on the plane, nothing was off limits, we vulnerably shared with one another, each trusting our instincts to be 100% transparent, knowing it was safe.

When dinner was finished, we slowly walked to the parking lot. I placed my hand on his back, ready to say goodbye, knowing he would not kiss me—he was too nervous. "I really enjoyed myself," I said.

He brought his hand to his brow rubbed his temple and blurted, "I'm sorry. I've never done this."

"Done what?" I asked.

"Date—I've never really dated. I was a gymnast in high school and college and spent every waking minute either in the gym or studying, so there wasn't really time for girls. Then, I met my wife in my first year of college. Other than a one-night stand, I've only ever been with her."

I stared back at him, my lips pressed together. How could a man this handsome, smart, successful, and kind be so incredibly pure? Little Jana whispered in my ear—*Go ahead*.

I leaned forward, stood on tiptoe, and pecked him on the lips. He pulled away, looked me in the eye, and smiled. "That was a little awkward," he said. "Can we try that again?"

I nodded.

He leaned in and looked deeply into my eyes. We kept the connection as he softly and slowly pressed his lips onto mine, holding for a second longer. We giggled and looked away from one another; a rush of energy flooded my body.

The second kiss was perfect.

*Chapter 38*

# BELOVED

*2015*

*"Oh Beloved, take me.*
*Liberate my soul.*
*Fill me with your love and release me from the two worlds.*
*If I set my heart on anything but you let fire burn me from inside.*
*Oh Beloved,*
*take away what I want.*
*Take away what I do.*
*Take away what I need.*
*Take away everything*
*that takes me from you."*[17]

—Rumi

I placed one foot in front of the other. My boot caught on a loose rock as I navigated the trail. I looked over at Lance who stayed by my side, though his natural gait would have put him several paces ahead of

---

17  Rumi, The Essential Rumi, ed. Coleman Barks (Harper Collins, 1995)

me. It was the Sunday after our first date, and he'd asked me to take him to my favorite trail. I decided to take him to Aspen Vista with my happy, panting fur babies trotting at our sides. It was a perfect fall day on Santa Fe Mountain—as we crested a hill and looked out over the landscape, the aspens came alive. The sky was a brilliant cobalt, set against the golden trees, the leaves like gold coins dancing in the soft breeze. I stood close enough to Lance to feel his energy. He gave off an ethereal warmth I wanted to grab onto and never let go.

As we turned from the lookout point and made our way back to the path, he looked over at me and smiled, his upper lip flecked with tiny glimmers of sweat. We'd barely made it fifty paces down before he stopped and reached for my hand, bringing it to his chest. The thuds were so intense against my palm, I looked up at him and asked, "Do you have a heart condition?"

"No!" he replied with a laugh. "My heart is racing because I'm so nervous."

I laughed, keeping my hand against his chest.

"I'm having such deep feelings for you, Jana."

I looked up at him, the dappled sun dancing across his face. Leaves pattered softly as a breeze swept through the trees. That's when I felt her—Little Jana seeking shelter behind my back, quietly peeking at Lance, unsure. I drew a breath, knowing I needed to protect and honor her. "I feel very intense feelings too, Lance. But you need to know that I am not becoming intimate again until I'm with the man I'll marry."

His lips turned up at the edges, a soft smile. "I understand."

After that day, Lance and I became inseparable. Whenever time allowed, he would make the hour drive up to Santa Fe. We would find a spot in a romantic old adobe restaurant feeding each other bites of food, take long hikes, or go horseback riding at Ghost Ranch where the iconic Georgia O'Keefe lived and painted. When our bodies grazed one another, *excitement*. When he took my hand in his, *peace and safety would flood me*.

When he told me he loved me, I would feel so much *joy and bliss*. For the first time, I was experiencing what it was like to be with *my man*. Though I'd only known him a short time, Lance was someone who fit so well into my world that I could hardly remember life before him.

One evening, Lance brought a pile of dry wood into my house and knelt in front of the fireplace, arranging the pile then setting it alight. He sat down on the couch, and I curled into him, my feet tucked beneath me as I pulled a soft blanket over our laps. As the fire pulsed, I looked up at Lance, who was staring into the flames, an easy smile spread across his face. "I have to show you something," I said.

I stood up and stepped over to my desk, grabbed my journal, and thumbed through the pages as I walked back to his side. I handed him my journal and said, "I want you to read this—it's my desire statement for my ideal partner." I had been certified to teach this Law of Attraction tool since 2003, I was nervous to share it with him, yet the more we were together, I knew I had attracted the exact man and relationship I desired.

He began to read. "Well, what do you think?" I asked, watching his eyes trace the page. His smile grew wider; his cheeks flushing pink from time to time. I knew exactly why—he was reading a list of the exact qualities he possessed.

Once he finished reading, he gazed into my eyes and laughed, "Well, I missed the age requirement by one year! Damn!"

I laughed and said, "Of course I'll take younger!"

My desire statement for my ideal partner:

*"I am in the process of attracting and allowing all that I need to do, to know, and to have so that I can attract and allow the perfect masculine partner into my life.*

*I'm overjoyed at the thought of being with a man who is a leader with clarity of purpose and vision, a man who has impeccable integrity and is honest, thoughtful, and caring.*

*Imagining myself exchanging ideas and inspiration with a man who is tuned into his emotions and articulates his feelings from a place of complete acceptance and surrender, I feel lit up. I feel free being with a man who celebrates my beauty and allows space in our togetherness.*

*It excites me to think about being with a man who is generous, altruistic, open minded and expansive, igniting ideas and inspiration to make a difference in our life and in the world.*

*I love knowing that this man is stable, clear minded and grounded in spiritual practices like meditation, yoga, being in nature and other sacred rituals. Envisioning myself with a man who is interested in mind body medicine and integrative health practices brings me a sense of alignment.*

*When I imagine being in a relationship with a man where we are supporting one another to let the relationship be a catalyst for us to express our full potential and creativity, I feel overjoyed.*

*Seeing myself with a man who gives himself permission to feel and doesn't anesthetize his feelings with temporary cheap external distractions, brings me peace and stability.*

*Imagining I am with a man who is 100% responsible for his life and the results he is creating feels liberating. There is little or no conflict in our relationship because neither of us take on an accusatory victim role.*

*My intentions and desires have Infinite organizing powers and God is orchestrating and unfolding all that needs to happen to bring about my desires. This or something greater. And So It Is!"*

## *Chapter 39*

---

# LOVE, FOUR WAYS
### ⤏ *2015* ⤎

Although Lance was my 'Dr. McDreamy', I knew that I had to take things slowly. He was going through a divorce, and I had no intention of being physically intimate with him until we had shared enough time together—not until, I was *sure*. Lance remained the perfect gentleman, rushing to open doors for me, gently placing his hand on my lower back, guiding me through tight crowds. He'd cook for me, hold me close, kiss my forehead and whisper *you're beautiful*. He never imposed himself on me or pushed me to become intimate. He kept enough distance to make me feel honored yet remained close enough to let me know he desired me. I remained cautious as well, being mindful not be seductive and use my sexuality to charm him. Our connection was pure.

As fall began to show early signs of winter, I sat on my couch petting Bonita. I was piecing together a few things Lance said—a few nearly imperceptible details from conversations we'd had on long walks on the trails. His words echoed in my ears: *My ex is requesting a legal separation—it's not what I wanted, but it's what she's asked for.* I sat straight up and thought, *Lance hadn't actually filed for divorce.*

My breath hastened.

My heart pounded.

Little Jana screamed, *Stop, stop, stop!*

I closed my eyes—I could see her clear as day. She stood in front of me stomping, her secondhand shoes banging the floor.

*He's going to hurt us!*

My mouth went dry.

My palms began to sweat.

*You promised you'd never let a man come in and rip our heart out! You promised I was your number one!*

I squeezed my eyes closed.

*"STOP!"*

My eyes sprang open, and I reached for my phone, dialing Lance without a second thought.

"Hi!" he answered.

"Lance, something is tugging at my heart, and I need to talk to you about it, now."

"Okay," he responded, his voice flush with concern.

"I just realized something—I was thinking through conversations and revisiting some talks we've had and—well, I didn't know that you weren't actually in the process of a divorce. You're only at the beginning. You haven't even filed yet."

"I hear you, Jana, and I promise you that—"

I cut him off, "No, I can't continue to date you until you've filed and are further down the path of the divorce."

"I understand. Please know, I have no intention of going back. I'm a man of integrity. I will move this forward."

"When you've taken action, you can call me and we can continue to date, but until then, I need you to respect my wishes." Without waiting for a goodbye, I took the phone from my ear and ended the call. I leaned back on the couch, took a deep breath—Little Jana was now quiet. I curled myself into a tight ball and allowed myself to grieve but found solace in the fact that I'd done something miraculous. I'd advocated for myself in a way that I never had before. I was proving that I would never allow anyone to fracture the relationship I was cultivating with my little girl.

Four days after that conversation, Lance filed for divorce.

In the days that followed, I was working with a client, facilitating a private intensive. When we were taking a break, I glanced at my phone, noticing a text as it popped up:

Lance: *Can I come up and hang at your house while you finish your sessions?*

Jana: *Sure!*

When I returned home that evening, I was energized. My private, intensive, one-on-one work was in high demand. I had dozens of inquiries each week but was only able to accommodate fifteen to twenty clients each year. My work with private clients always brings me such joy, I vibrate for hours, even after the most difficult sessions.

I opened the door, noticing an auric glow coming from the kitchen. I walked inside and Lance was standing there behind the table upon which he had arranged fresh, cut flowers. I looked around in awe, bringing my hands to my cheeks. My house was immaculate—there were lit candles and the sounds of a saxophone floating through the house. "I have a gift for you," he said enthusiastically. He handed me a piece of paper with "Love, Four Ways" scrawled across the top.

### Love, Four Ways

*The innocent love of children.*

*I remember a girl that sat in front of me in kindergarten. She was cute, tough, smart and confident. I felt something for her that I did not feel for any of the other girls. I wanted her attention. I wanted her to pretend marry me. I feel the same way about you. My love for you is innocent and pure like that first crush. I want your attention and I want you to pretend to marry me (for now). I love you like my Little Lance would love your Little Jana.*

*The passionate love of young adults.*
*I want to love every part of you with every part of me. I want to caress you, tickle you, kiss you and lick you. I want to make love to you so that you scream in ecstasy. I want our lovemaking to leave you spent in a heap of bliss. I will pleasure you with intimate, physical love when the time is right.*

*The graceful love of elders.*
*I love the look I see in some old couples' faces. It is clear in how their eyes smile when they look at one another, that they have been in love for a very long time. They know what each other are thinking, they can order each other's food and they complete each other's sentences. They are connected in a deep spiritual way. They are so connected that when one of them dies, the other is usually not far behind. They cannot be separated for very long, even by death. I love you like a doddering old man loves his beautiful old wife.*

*The love that is not of this Earth.*
*This is the love that has made me believe in God. The other three are familiar to me. I have experienced them in some ways. The spiritual love that I feel for you cannot be explained by Earthly words or concepts. You knew that love like this existed. I could not have even imagined that a love like this could exist. I love you in a way that makes me know that we are all connected and there is Divinity. That Divinity is in us and in our love.*

I slid into one of my dining chairs where I sat with tears streaming down my face. I looked up at Lance—the tears in his eyes picking up flecks of warm light. He leaned down and whispered, "You are my beloved and I am yours – always."

Little Jana jumped for joy, tugging at my arm.

*Our beloved—we've found him.*

*Chapter 40*

# CO-COMMITMENT

## 2016

There is an inherent electricity that is common when falling deeply in love. I relished it all. The excitement of being with Lance was, at times, overwhelming. I felt myself leaving my body and watching the scenes unfold, it was as if it were too much goodness for me to take in. I was acutely aware of old beliefs that had the possibility of resurfacing, yet they rarely did. My internal conversation with myself was encouraging, I knew I had worked my entire life to attract a relationship like this one. In moments when I once may have faltered, I remained steady. At times when I may have become nervous and ran, I remained still. I felt nothing but safety with Lance. My heart belonged to him.

I put my car in park in front of the restaurant, my heart beaming. As I stepped out of my car and hurried toward the entrance, a rare breeze caught my hair and tickled my face. The dry Ojai air was delicious, the lush valley is filled with minerals that swirl up and flavor the air. I scurried through the door and was greeted by the smell of garlic and basil, mingled with soft notes of leather. I gazed past the host just as Lance stood to greet me with a kiss. "It's so good to see you," he said with a smile, pulling my chair out for me.

"Thank you," I said, scooting it in.

Lance took his seat and stared across the table at me. "Is it crazy that I'm chasing you all over the country?"

"Of course not. I love it." I beamed.

As I prepared for my spring San Diego retreat, I had the idea to ask Lance to co-facilitate. I had been consistently leading group retreats each year since 2004. I was teaching the Emotional Healing System to students in Denmark, France, Saudi Arabia, Australia and all throughout North America. Over the years, my retreats had evolved from teaching meditation, shadow work, and forgiveness processes, to now including inner child work, reparenting, and powerful envisioning processes. I was fascinated with quantum physics and how science validates spirituality and transformation. Lance wanted to share what he knew of neuroplasticity, epigenetics, and all the geeky stuff that happens in the human body when it's in the process of change. His knowledge was the perfect counterpart to mine, and I knew it would give participants a beautiful, layered experience. He was thrilled that I asked him to co-lead with me, yet he was always so humble and never wanted to take any attention away from me.

In the glow of the restaurant's soft lighting, I held Lance's stare as he reached across the table for my hand. I reached out and met his palm with mine—his soft grasp felt like home. He opened his eyes wide. "Where did you come from?" He asked.

"Your fantasies," I immediately answered.

It was a fun question we asked each other from time to time, reminding each other that our relationship was extraordinary.

When I would ask Lance, "Where did you come from?"

He'd immediately answer, "You ordered me up from the Universe!"

Several weeks later, my travel finally slowed. Lance and I were back in our rhythm in New Mexico, moving through life together—twin souls becoming reunited. As if the Universe was following a script to support us in moving forward, our leases were up on the same date. We took it as a *sign* and decided to move in together.

I began looking for houses that would be near his sons, since they were still in high school, and he needed to be near them. I would make the compromise by moving closer to Albuquerque. I still had my healing center in Santa Fe and would commute there when I was hosting a client.

In my search, I came upon what I thought was a great house in an area outside of Albuquerque. I set up a tour with our realtor, and Lance went with me. Together, hand-in-hand, we walked from room to room, feeling the energy of the space, imagining our life unfolding within those walls. I liked the flow of the home and found its energy calming. Lance seemed to like it too, so I put down a deposit and began to handle paperwork, contracts, and more with our realtor.

The next evening, Lance and I had gone to one of his sons' basketball games, and as we drove home, Lance was behaving in a way I hadn't seen before. The air in the car was thick with tension, the streetlights sending bursts of light through the car like small bolts of lightning.

"What's wrong?" I asked.

"Nothing," he answered, never glancing in my direction.

A lump formed in my throat—Little Jana tugged at me.

*Something is wrong.*

I was committed to the microscopic truth – telling the truth is sexy was my motto. I shook my head. "Okay, well, something is going on. I need you to tell me the truth."

He was silent.

"I'm just going to go home tonight—I need some space to process."

The next day, as the earth woke, the gravel of my driveway popped beneath Lance's tires. I opened the door for him. "Hi, do you want coffee?" I asked.

"No thanks," he replied, coming inside. He sat down on the couch and motioned for me to sit next to him. His eyes were red-rimmed. "I felt abandoned by you when you left last night."

"I hear you," I responded, placing my hand on his knee. "I believe we teach people how to treat us, and I'm helpless over you. Something was wrong last night—and I can see it's still troubling you now. I just need you to talk to me."

"You're right. I—I have to be honest." He stammered, "I don't like the house."

"The house?"

"Yes, I don't want to rent that house—I don't like the area, I don't like the layout, I don't see us living there."

I leaned into him. "Why didn't you say something?"

". . . I was afraid you'd break up with me because you liked it so much. I thought it was too late since we already put down a deposit."

That's when I recognized it—my heart saw his—this was an unconscious pattern he was replaying.

He sniffed and leaned into me, placing his arms around me, burying his head into my shoulder. We both cried, his tears slid down my shoulder and settled in the crook of my arm. "Listen. You feel abandoned because you abandoned a part of yourself when you refused to be open with me. You shut down Little Lance. But your responsibility is to him, the same way mine is to Little Jana."

He nodded.

"You need to listen to *his* needs first and foremost. That's what I do. I listen to Little Jana first. I want us to be in a co-committed relationship and to support one another as we honor ourselves too."

Lance sat upright and opened his hands. I reached forward and wrapped my arms around him.

"I love you," he said and kissed my forehead.

I stood up and went to my desk, grabbing a notebook and a pen. "Forget that rental. Let's script out our ideal house."

For the next hour, steaming cups of coffee in-hand, Lance and I worked together, listing out everything we wanted in our perfect home. We started on the outside with landscape, surrounding trees, the views, then walked the floorplan, room by room, scribbling everything we could possibly want in a home. Within days of writing out the desire statement, we found a beautiful, brand-new home to rent with a magnificent view of Sandia Peak. We signed the lease immediately and moved forward, taking our next step as a couple.

*Chapter 41*

# THE WILLOW TREE
## 2017

For the next two years, Lance and I moved through life balancing being close and taking space. In conscious relationships, space is healthy. Lance was struggling through turbulent challenges in the divorce process, but through it all, we became even stronger. With each valley, there was a peak hiding just around the corner, and we navigated it all with ease, using the tools we teach. Our relationship was smooth sailing; we'd take long hikes with the fur babies that were no longer just mine, they were ours. We'd lay tangled up fireside, and sway to the silky sounds of Jazz while sumptuous dinners simmered on the stove. Our love felt unique. It felt other worldly.

As time progressed, we talked about marriage. But not in dreamy tones, like something you trace and retrace in your mind that will never actually happen. Instead, we'd sit, swirling margaritas, or nestled on the couch and would discuss what kind of plan might suit us—what kind of celebration felt like the love we shared. We discussed how cool it would be to get married on the anniversary of the day that we met on the plane. We pondered eloping to the lake region of Northern Italy, marrying in an old, beautiful villa on Lake Como, just the two of us.

We shared our thoughts with our children—we always wanted to keep them in the know. It was his sons, Kellen and Nico, who intervened and shared that they wanted to be a part of that special day for their dad. "You're so different now, Dad," they'd say. "You're happier than we've ever seen you."

As their words washed over me, it became clear. We didn't need to escape to far corners of the earth, to huddle together and keep our eternal love between us. No. We needed to allow the official joining of our souls to envelop those we loved most—our kids. Instead of flying across the world to marry, we would choose a place that was incredibly special to us both—Taos. We'd join together under the giant willow trees, on the original ceremonial grounds of the Tiwa people from the Taos pueblo. It was a perfect location for us to stand before our family, surrounded by the splendor of nature, and say our sacred vows. With our perfect plans in place, I waited patiently. There was one last detail—one tiny thing I couldn't control—Lance's proposal. Little Jana smiled wide, her sweet smile reflecting the thrill of my own anticipation.

*We've found our beloved.*

*Chapter 42*

# ON BENDED KNEE
### 2017

The mountains were silhouetted against the deep blue sky, the sun still sleepy, nestled below the horizon. I walked to the passenger side of the car and slid in, leaning back onto the headrest, closing my eyes, still heavy with sleep. Lance placed my bags in the trunk and jumped into the driver's side, sitting down hard in his seat. "Ready?" he asked.

I was heading to Banff for a retreat with Deepak organized by the Chopra Center. I was going to miss Lance, but I was incredibly excited. It had been a few years since I attended an event with my teacher—the man whose teachings had guided me like a beacon for the past 25 years.

We made our way down the long gravel driveway, and pulled onto the main road, then the highway. Soft music rolled from the speakers as Lance placed his hand on my knee for the drive. Lance pulled into short term parking, put the car in park, quickly moving around the car to open my door and help me step onto the sidewalk. He pulled my bag behind him with his left hand while taking my hand in his right. He always insists on walking me into the airport, nervous when I travel alone. It's sweet. I clutched his hand tightly, squeezing harder every so often.

After checking my bag and getting my boarding pass, we headed toward security. As we rode the escalator up to the second floor, my mind wandered briefly to that fateful day nearly two years prior, running to this same escalator toward my future. I rested my head on his shoulder as we glided.

When we stepped off the escalator, Lance grabbed my arm and pulled me to the side, away from the steady stream of people headed to security. He looked me in the eyes, dropping down to one knee.

My heart was light as a feather.

Little Jana was dancing with glee.

Looking up at me, Lance's eyes caught the light. He pulled a box from his pocket and opened it, revealing the most beautiful, radiant, Asscher-cut, yellow sapphire surrounded with smaller diamonds, clear as ice.

I brought my hand to my chest, my cheeks turning bright pink.

He smiled and asked, "Jana, will you be my beloved forever? Will you marry me?"

With a few people now craning their necks to get a better view, I shouted, "Yes!"

After he placed the ring on my finger, he swept me into a deep hug, lifting me off my feet. He kissed my lips, put me down, leaned in and whispered, "Always and in all ways."

## Chapter 43

# HAPPILY, EVER AFTER
### ∽ 2017 ∾

Our wedding was perfect. It was late August; the monsoons came, first in big, fat drops, then in sheets that blotted out the sun. Thunder rumbled and big bolts of lightning illuminated the sky. Rain on your wedding day is thought to be a blessing—the cleansing rains washing away the difficulties of the past. In Hindu traditions, rain on the day of a wedding is said to make the couple even stronger and longer lasting; a wet knot is difficult to untie. It was magical. The smell of the earth musty and wet; the light filtering through the clouds; the patter of leaves as the wind whirled through the trees; the babbling of the river rushing over rocks. As I took my place across from Lance, Little Jana beamed. I anchored the moment with a deep inhale and silently acknowledged my truth: this is the moment I have been waiting for all my life.

I stared into Lance's eyes as the officiant began to speak, reading the vows we had written to align with the principles of our purpose as a couple.

The officiant said, "Do you promise to see all circumstances as an opportunity to help you grow, to open your hearts, to accept yourselves, and each other; and to generate compassion for others who are suffering?"

*We do.*

"Do you promise to seek to understand yourselves, each other, and all living beings, to examine your own minds continually and to regard all the mysteries of life with curiosity and joy?"

*We do.*

"Do you promise to preserve and enrich your affection for each other, and to share it with all beings?"

*We do.*

"Do you promise to take the loving feelings you have for one another and your vision of each other's potential and inner beauty as an example and to radiate this love outwards to all beings?"

*We do.*

Then, we invited Taylor, Kellen and Nico to share their feelings about our marriage. Taylor stood next to me and shared first, "When I was a little girl, I always dreamed my mom would find a man worthy of her." She swept a tear from her cheek, looked over at Lance, and said, "I'm so happy that my mom found you and I'm so proud to call you my stepdad."

Kellen and Nico, each stood and spoke eloquently from their hearts, sharing how much it meant to them to witness their dad so happy.

As Lance and I leaned in to kiss one another, it was as if I'd finally completed the circle. My Wise Little One remained at my side, jumping for joy as Lance held my face in his hands and whispered, "I love you."

As if we needed another auspicious sign after the monsoon, there was a total solar eclipse the very next day—August 21$^{st}$, 2017. It was visible throughout the entire United States. A total solar eclipse holds incredible significance—it means all possibilities are on the table. The rare event points to bold, confident changes, leading to long term success. At every turn, Lance and I were being reminded that we have all the support of the Universe on our side.

# EPILOGUE

s Lance and I settled into married life together, my mom remained a steady presence in our lives. She continued to struggle with mental illness, never seeking traditional or non-traditional methods to heal. It was as if she felt comfort in her internal chaos—it was familiar, safe in a way. Her house became her cocoon; she rarely left, maintaining a pattern of sleep, reading, gardening, and more sleep. We spoke often, but our conversations were short—clipped.

In the final years of her life, her mind began to falter. The disease crept further into her mind and began to choke out the essence of who she was at her core. Mom was beginning to disappear.

One day, my phone rang, it was Mom. When I answered, her voice was broken. She was crying repeating over and over, "I'm scared Jana." She managed to heave out "I need help. I can't remember how to pay my bills. I left the fire on the stove and burned a pot."

I didn't hesitate—I jumped right in to take care of her. After all, that's what Little Jana vowed to do.

*One day, I'll take care of you.*

The last years of Mom's life were difficult for Roy and me. The responsibility was immense, and our relationship suffered. I slipped into old patterns trying to navigate it with ease. Our spiritual values were vastly different. Roy and I had grown so far apart, the only thing we had in common was our childhood traumas. I used all the tools in my spiritual toolbox, but sometimes still found myself tangled. As adults we aren't required to stay in unhealthy relationships with family simply because they are family. I stood strong with my Wise Little One, surrendering to a time of great pain and helplessness.

The last time Mom and I were together, two weeks before she passed, I laid in bed with her, snuggled up like a child. Together, we rested in the flickering glow of old black and white westerns on TV. She stroked my arm lovingly; I nuzzled into her bony frame. Although she was in late-stage Alzheimer's, one truth remained with her at all times. I looked up at her and asked, "Do you know who I am?"

She smiled and said, "You are my sunshine."

Mom took her last breath July 23, 2022. She was at peace, cradled within the stars and nebulas where I'd once found myself, long ago.

When I reflect on my life and all the chaos, conflict, and trauma that I endured, I know that it was all by Divine Order. From that early awakening at age twelve, I have come to know this Truth; I am a Soul having this human experience in order to learn and grow. I have been gifted with every person and circumstance in my life. Each and every one has invited me to strengthen my spiritual connection, to deepen my understanding of myself and create a beautiful life.

In the eight years we have been together, Lance and I have sailed through his divorce, the deaths of both of our mothers, moves, and job changes. With each crashing wave, we are reminded that our love is a balm that soothes the pain and heartbreak life throws at us. Our love is pure, with very little conflict, and although not perfect, it's been damn close. It's *wabi-sabi*; the word in Japanese used to describe the perfection in the imperfection.

"From everyone who has been given much, much will be demanded; and from the one who has been entrusted with much, much more will be asked."[18] Jesus spoke these words explaining that when we are blessed it is expected that we use the blessings to serve and benefit others. Lance and I feel an obligation to share our gifts and talents with the world. We are here on this planet to leave it better than we found it.

And, in all things, I am guided by a presence once small and timid, now bright, bold, and free. She is a beam of light in the darkness; a bright, luminous star on a moonless night. I put her first in all things. I honor her with every breath I take. I am hers, and she is mine.

*Wise Little One*.

---

18 New International Version, Luke 12:48 (2011) BibleGateway.com. https://www.biblegate-
way.com/passage/?search=Luke%2012&version=NIV

# ACKNOWLEDGMENTS

Writing a book about the story of your life is a surreal process. There were many peaks and valleys. First and foremost, I'm forever grateful to Alee Anderson, for her editorial genius, sensitive spirit, understanding of trauma, and ongoing support in bringing my stories to life. Kristen Ingebretson, for a beautifully crafted book cover, who knew so much goes into the cover of a book! Asya Blue for designing an artfully designed interior with all the decorative details.

Printed in the USA
CPSIA information can be obtained
at www.ICGtesting.com
LVHW041832300823
756735LV00003B/306

9 798987 549728